# Martin Larson's Best

*Selected Articles from the*

*Popular Weekly Column*

*"Our World in Conflict"*

*in The SPOTLIGHT*

Library of Congress Catalog Card No.: 84-052843

ISBN 0-935036-06-7

300 INDEPENDENCE AVE., S.E.
WASHINGTON, D. C.    20003

# TABLE OF CONTENTS

# *INTRODUCTION*

Dr. Martin A. Larson's weekly column, "Our World in Conflict," continues to be one of the most popular features in The SPOTLIGHT. In it he assails the complexities and inequities of the Internal Revenue Code, government spending and waste, and related subjects in his inimitable style and unimpeachable scholarship.

In response to popular demand, the first compilation of such columns, *How You Can Save Money On Your Taxes This Year*, appeared in 1978. That work was revised in 1982.

This fourth printing has been updated through 1984 to take advantage of much new material, especially articles relating to important legislative and judicial developments, as well as administrative regulations.

New chapters are included on Jefferson, the Federal Reserve, inflation, and related matters.

This new volume will help the average taxpayer discover his fundamental rights and benefits. He will be better able to deal with the IRS from a position of strength, escape entrapments, resist pressures, and defend himself against the bureaucracy.

He will also better understand the ramifications of the threatening government colossus—in spite of all the non-partisan political promises to "balance the budget." Several articles deal with the monstrous Social Security program—and how it could be replaced by a universal trust plan with enormous advantages, permitting tens of millions of "free, self-reliant individuals (to be) secure in their economic and political lives."

We are glad to offer this latest edition, knowing it will find great usefulness in the days ahead among a multitude of Dr. Larson's fans.

January, 1985

Bernard R. DeRemer  
Executive Secretary  
LIBERTY LOBBY

# Ch. 1
# Tax Rebellion:
# Techniques and Victories

# *Vivien Kellems — Pioneer Tax Rebel*

The redoubtable Vivien Kellems, whose book "Toil, Taxes and Trouble," tells the story of her 1948 battle with the IRS, was another pioneer in the great battle against federal income taxation. However, it must be noted that neither she nor others challenged the constitutionality of the IR Code; nor did they demand the end of federal income taxation—only its basic reform.

As owner of the Cable Grip Co., she refused to withhold income taxes from the pay of her employees, saying that she would not serve as an unpaid tax-collector. Even though her employees had paid their own taxes, the IRS seized $8,000 from her account, which she forced the agency to return after a jury trial. The IRS then added a new section to the Code [3402(d)] which provides that employers need not collect and transmit income taxes so long as the employees pay them directly; however, if they do not, the employer becomes fully liable.

Miss Kellems in due course achieved national publicity by advocating equality of taxation for single and married persons. However, her greatest battle occured in 1969-70, when she refused to show her records to the IRS without a proper 4th Amendment warrant. On Dec. 16, 1969, she was ordered by Judge Canella of the U.S. District Court to surrender her records. When she neither complied nor appealed, she was hauled before Judge Zampano on Feb. 25, 1970, in the U.S. District Court of New Haven, Conn. Here she represented herself in opposition to a team of high-powered government lawyers, who attempted to trick her into stating under oath that her return was fraudulent. She declared that she did not need to perjure herself in order to take the 5th Amendment.

On April 10, 1970, Johnnie M. Walters, then assistant attorney general of the tax division of the Department of Justice, declared in a letter addressed to the Court that Miss Kellems had properly invoked her 5th Amendment privilege and that all criminal charges were to be dismissed. And so the IRS admitted officially that it cannot enforce its summons to produce records even under court order.

The IRS then disallowed Miss Kellems' unverified deductions and presented her with a heavy assessment. However, she greeted this levy with scorn; and from that day until her death she never made another return or paid a penny in taxes. She had become what is known as a "sensitive case," and was therefore left alone.

She died on Jan. 25, 1977, at the age of 78. The New York "Times" published a long resume of her life, but interestingly enough, while relating various insignificant details, never even mentioned her last great battle with, and landmark victory over, the IRS.

# Austin Flett vs. 'Lack of Jurisdiction'

One of the earliest pioneers in the Tax-Rebellion was Austin Flett of Chicago. Working for an insurance company, he discovered as early as 1942 that tax-exempt mutuals could undersell his taxpaying firm; and for several years he devoted himself to a study of some 12 million tax-free, unaudited exempts, such as foundations, co-ops, churches, and many other sacred cows which, in his opinion, unlawfully escaped taxes totalling billions of dollars annually on business income.

In 1956 and 1958, he paid a tax under protest; thereafter, and for the remainder of his life, he not only filed in blank, but demanded huge sums from the government as fees for information concerning tax-dodgers; in 1959, he demanded $5 million; in 1961, $25 million; and in 1966, $50 million. He offered to assist the U.S. Treasury in collecting these sums.

After losing his job in 1958-59, he went up and down the United States lecturing to all and sundry who would listen to his message.

In 1965, the IRS brought suit against Flett, demanding $5,010. He did not pay, nor was he brought to trial. Instead, he intensified his crusade and filed a countersuit demanding $48 million, including interest.

In 1966, the IRS filed a criminal information against him for failing to file a proper return; when the Service offered a compromise settlement, he rejected this with withering scorn.

The Service went to extreme lengths to discover and document his income; and, since he said that, over the years, IRS harassment had cost him $200,000, he must have had substantial income; however, since this could not be established by the rules of evidence, the IRS was helpless in its attempt to bring a successful criminal prosecution.

When the IRS forced Flett's safety box, only papers condemning the agency as a Communist conspiracy were found in it.

In 1969, the government ordered Flett to report to a government hospital for a psychiatric examination. Instead, he went to Washington, and conferred with various congressmen and other government officials, and, instead of obeying the order, he sued the officials who sought to have him incarcerated for civil damages in the amount of $2 million for conspiring to deprive him of his civil rights under sections 241 and 242 of Title 18, U.S. Code. The suit was dismissed "for lack of jurisdiction."

Flett never paid a penny of income taxes during the last 13 years of his life. He lectured to thousands of people. The government was never able to lay a hand on him. His life ended on June 12, 1971, when, applause ringing in his ears, he sank dead into his chair as he completed an address to the Arizona Breakfast Club in Phoenix.

Even then he was not aware of what a progeny of dragon's teeth he had sown.

# Taxpayers' Rights

I have awaited with considerable interest reactions from people who have used my manual and service, "How To Defend Yourself Against The IRS."* I would indeed be sorry and feel useless if this did not serve its purpose to subscribers. However, I know from first-hand reports that a number have found it valuable.

I recall in particular one lady from a New England state who kept calling me and giving me a blow-by-blow description of developments in her case. The IRS had called, demanding that at a certain hour two or three days later she be prepared to exhibit all documents including cancelled checks, that a brash agent demanded.

But she had read my book, and calmly told the gentleman that no communication would take place except in writing. Therefore, the agent was compelled to write; and declared that in a couple of days he would be at her house to examine everything and implied the direst consequences if she were to fail in complete compliance.

She wrote that she would not be able to have all materials on hand at that time. He then wrote that he would be at her door at a certain time and that she had better be there, ready and prepared. When he arrived, someone else answered the door (after all, she had not agreed to an appointment); the agent was told that the lady had been called out of town and that a later date would have to be arranged for a conference.

Well, finally a date was agreed upon. When the man came to her house, he faced not only the intended victim, but also three of her friends. When he declared that they could not remain, she read Publication 556† to him, which so subdued the man that he seemed at once to develop a new and more humble personality.

He then asked to examine all documents necessary to verify deductions and the lady spoke somewhat as follows:

"Sir, I have made full disclosure under penalties of perjury; I have paid all the taxes due. If I have made any misstatement, I can be prosecuted for felony, and the burden of proof is on the government. I will not show you any records unless I am forced to do so by final judicial authority.

"If you disallow any of my deductions, I will carry this case through the District Office and to the appellate level, and if necessary, all the way to the Tax Court, which, as you know, will take a lot of our time, both yours and mine. But you will never get another penny from me unless you prove that I owe it."

And what happened? The agent went back to his office, where he must have discussed this courageous lady at some length. Anyway, they went over her return very carefully, and found a slight error in addition, which required a small payment, which she admitted was due and which she paid. And that was the end of it.

There was no audit; no questions were answered, no documents were shown.

What might have happened following an audit, we do not know. IRS agents often invent provisions in the tax laws which do not exist there and they make interpretations which even Solomon could not understand.

A courageous and determined lady won another victory for the taxpayers!

*Available for $175 from Government Educational Foundation, Box 1622, Washington, D.C. 20013. Price includes automatic subscription to all supplements and changes for three years from date of order.
†"Audit of Returns, Appeal Rights, and Claims for Refund"—available from any IRS office.

# *Amish Artisans and Farmers*

**There is nothing that sends the cold shivers up and down the spines of the** Washington bureaucrats as does the thought that some day there will be a united refusal on the part of the American people to knuckle under to their dictates; and, since they know that it is in the power of the self-employed middle class to do just that, they regard its members as their greatest potential enemy.

That such a refusal is within the grasp of this economic segment in our society is demonstrated conclusively by the victory of a comparatively small number of determined individuals. The farmers and artisans who make up the Beachy and the Old Order of the Amish Church societies comprise altogether about 19,000 individuals (perhaps 4,000 or 5,000 families) and are found largely in Pennsylvania and Ohio. As a unit, all of these **simply refused to pay any Social Security taxes; however, since their progenitors in Switzerland, Germany, and** elsewhere had endured imprisonment, flogging, exile, confiscation of property, even death, and many other forms of persecution, nothing that the IRS or any other federal agency could do was sufficient to force even the slightest compliance. The government placed liens on their real estate and seized their horses, wagons, livestock, poultry, and household goods; but their resistance only became more adamant and determined. Finally, the bureaucrats threw up their hands in despair and surrender.

**Since it was obviously impossible to compel obedience and since it was** not, at least yet, expedient to shoot or imprison entire populations for asserting a basic right, the bureaucrats devised a face-saving scheme: they inserted Section 1402(g) — effective **December 31, 1976 — into the Code which, without mentioning the Amish** by name spells out provisions under which lay members of this society — but none other — may abandon the Social Security system by filing Form 4029. Similarly in 1948, after its confrontation with Vivien Kellems, in order to avoid an adverse decision by the Supreme Court, the IRS inserted Section 3402(d) into the Code, which provides that if an employee pays all Social Security taxes demanded, the employer cannot be forced to collect and transmit the same.

As Jefferson once stated, when its time has come, an idea can spread **with lightning-like rapidity throughout the masses of the people. At the** present time, there are perhaps a few hundred highly vocal tax rebels in the United States (there were only two or three a few years ago), whom the government selects as specific targets for prosecution; but there are other millions, who, because of their low profile, are ignored. As inflation, taxes and the inevitable concomitant of federal extortion become more onerous and ever greater numbers become actual or imminently potential victims, the spirit of open revolt may quickly fill the minds and hearts of many millions.

When that day arrives, they need simply in unison do what the Amish did: declare that they will no longer pay for their own enslavement and destruction; and that will be the end of the Internal Revenue Service and will also herald the return to constitutional government in the United States.

Incidentally, as a good friend of mine has observed, is not the government guilty of unconstitutional discrimination when it confers upon one specific group of people a definite benefit which it denies to all others? Can the mere enumeration of certain qualifications sidestep or avoid the provisions of the Fourteenth Amendment of the Constitution?

# Evasion and Resistance

The manner in which the tax-revolt is proliferating is indeed wonderful to behold. I just heard a radio announcer declare that literally tens of thousands—especially in the construction industry—in seven western states have filed W-4 returns with the word "Exempt" on line 3—which means that the employer will not withhold any income taxes from the pay of such employees. The commentator added that unless these people make proper returns and pay their taxes on April 15, they can be in for a lot of trouble with the IRS.

On August 25, 1978, the Arizona "Republic" carried a feature article which stated that 3,000 people— many of whom had recently arrived in the state—are now under investigation for claiming total exemptions falsely on their W-4 forms. If this number are under investigation, we believe the actual number must be greater.

No doubt this development is driving the IRS "up the wall." William Bray, chief of the Collections Division in Arizona, states that people who file false withholding Allowance Certificates "may find themselves in jail or at least in a financial bind at next year's income-tax deadline."

Of all the empty threats I have ever heard, this is perhaps the most ridiculous. To put a citizen in jail for income-tax evasion requires an indictment, arrest, prosecution, trial and conviction—followed by appeals all the way to the Supreme Court—a process which costs the taxpayers many thousands of dollars and takes from four to seven years. How can the government complete such a process upon thousands or tens of thousands?

On the other hand, how can it collect assessments by civil procedures from people who have no real estate, bank accounts, or any other known asset beyond the clothes on their backs and perhaps an automobile not titled to them and therefore beyond the clutches of the tax-collector?

Bray admits that it "is not an employer's responsibility to make sure that employees are filing correct withholding statements." And so he suggests that "Arizonans who suspect they may have filed incorrect withholding forms contact IRS Taxpayer Assistance . . . Filing a false form can bring a year in prison and a $500 fine."

So said the spider to the fly. How many flies will flee to the spider for help—unwanted help?

The fact is that the IRS is growing more and more helpless and desperate in its attempts to deal with the various forms which the taxpayer revolt is taking. Proprietors who keep good-looking books which underreport income; thousands or millions of propertyless workers who file Exempt W-4 forms; and the vast army who now earn one or two unreported incomes or who have joined the "underground economy" are beyond the reach, control or reprisal of the IRS. If it attempts to deal with all of these, it will indeed have its hands full—not to mention its task of auditing some 3 million conventional returns every year.

And then, of course, we have the heroic constitutional patriots, a few of whom have become guests of our Uncle Sam for certain periods; these seem to be the only ones on whom the government can lay its talons. But some of these are winning signal victories in jury trials; even if they lose, they become symbols of heroic and patriotic resistance to tyranny.

# Tax Rebellion Statistics

I once heard a speaker declare that most of the American people belong in two categories so far as the federal income tax is concerned: rebels who refuse to file at all or people who do everything to reduce their income taxes by any possible method.

In fact, John Connally declared when he was the secretary of the treasury, that in the Southeast, 97 per cent of all returns prepared by others for taxpayers were fraudulent; and then, as if to pile Pelion upon Ossa, Johnny Walters declared that in other parts of the country, conditions were even worse.

In any event, there is no question that Americans are gradually learning to become as adept in defeating the IRS as their European counterparts, especially in France and Italy, became some years ago.

We had, in this country, in 1971, according to the 1974 "Statistical Abstract," (pp. 476-77) 9.7 million proprietorships, with total receipts of $255.2 billion—an average of $26,380—and net profits of $41 billion—an average of $4,210.

Of these, 9.2 million or 94.6 per cent had receipts of less than $100,000. There were 1.7 million retail establishments with reported receipts totalling $94.2 billion and profits of $5.9 billion. Revenues, therefore, averaged $53,420 and profits $3,357. There were 2 million service establishments with receipts totalling $92.4 billion and averaging $15,350; profits were $15.2 billion averaging $5,880.

We see, therefore, that in spite of Marxist predictions and attempts on the part of the federal bureaucracy to destroy it, small and independent business continues to exist and flourish; the number of such establishments increased from 5.5 million in 1945 to 10.1 million in 1972.

That the average business is comparatively small is obvious from the fact that reported gross income was only $53,420 even in retail stores and the net profits only $4,210. However, the receipts of the 9 million which averaged less than $100,000 totalled $130 billion, or 52 per cent of the total.

We believe that these small incomes can be explained only by assuming that small business generally and substantially under-reports its income. How can the IRS know, for example, whether a barber trims 15 or 20 heads on an average day? If an independent hardware or paint merchant grosses $125 or $150? If a 14-unit motel has an average of 6 or 10 occupied rooms an average night? Or whether a multitude of independent contractors are reporting their income fully or at all?

Since millions belong in these or similar categories, you can understand why the federal bureaucrats hate small and independent business and seek by any means to destroy it. Doctors, lawyers, merchants, service establishments and millions of other independents simply cannot be policed.

Let us assume that many of these make no returns at all or understate their income by 25 per cent. This would constitute an under-reporting of taxable income by about $40 billion and of perhaps $20 billion in income taxes. And this includes only one category—the self-employed.

We believe that the people of the United States are now escaping at least $30 and perhaps $40 billion in taxes by the general methods we have described. This, of course, is in addition to the legal tax-avoidance resulting from the loopholes in the Code which enable favored individuals and corporations to escape at least $70 billion in federal taxes.

# *How Taxes are Evaded*

According to an AP article, the IRS now states officially that for the year 1976, individuals failed to report income of somewhere between $75 and $100 billion, on which a tax of from $13 to $17 billion would have been paid—if reported. In addition, another $6 to $9 billion of taxes was evaded on income deriving from criminal activities which totaled somewhere between $25 and $35 billion. Such evasion, therefore, totaled $26 billion and constituted 18.2 percent of the $142 billion collected in personal income taxes in 1976.

Since the total personal income tax for 1978 was about $181.8 billion, the same rate of evasion would constitute a treasury loss of at least $33 billion. "The IRS," we are told, "estimated that the biggest group of scofflaws are self-employed persons . . . such workers failed to report between $33 and $39.5 billion in 1976 income. Other shortfalls involved under-reporting of wages and salaries of $27 billion; interest by $9.4 billion; and dividends by $4.7 billion." No wonder the IRS wants Social Security numbers on all 1099 forms!

The IRS promises, "in fairness to those who report their income and pay their tax to . . . strengthen its efforts to discover and tax unreported income."

The official report noted that "Voluntary reporting of income is very high where incomes are subject to withholding and much lower where incomes are subject to neither withholding or (sic) information reporting."

We need not be surprised, therefore, that the IRS does everything in its power to eliminate the middle class and to reduce everyone, except the rich and the super-rich, to the status of what the Marxists call wage-slaves.

The Internal Revenue Service offers these proposals:

● Better use of information documents, such as those filed by a waiter on his tips (and we presume the 1099s covering interest, dividends, rentals and royalties, as well as the 1096s covering contract payments);

● A computer program designed to help investigators determine which persons are most likely not to file income-tax returns; and

● Support for a Treasury Department proposal to withhold 10 percent of the payments businesses make to independent contractors.

However, we should point out that the IRS estimates of current evasion are far below what they undoubtedly know them to be. In 1973, when the agency admitted a loss of $5 billion, independent experts placed the true amount at not less than $25 billion. Now, in addition to the $75 or $100 billion which escapes legally because of loopholes, allowances, deductions, etc; and the losses from criminal and underworld activity; there is no doubt that the underground economy now accounts for a loss of at least $100 billion and under-reporting for at least an equal sum. Furthermore, the rapidly expanding business by barter and exchange (quite legal) is now certainly depriving the treasury of many billions in taxes annually.

And so the battle between the IRS and the middle class continues with increasing intensity and expansion.

# Millions of Non-Filers

We have known for years that the IRS fails annually to collect many billions of dollars due under its laws. We estimate that the treasury is losing at least $100 billion because of legal loopholes and at least an equal amount because of underreporting, outright fraud or simple failure or refusal to make reports or payments.

Now, according to a UPI release dated July 11, 1979, the government admits officially that it is losing untold billions every year because "some Americans neglect to file income tax returns and thus avoid detection by tax collectors . . ." In 1972, we are told, "the latest year for which statistics are available, some 5 million wage earners avoided payments of $2 billion in income taxes because they failed to send returns to the Internal Revenue Service and were never caught, according to a study of the General Accounting Office."

That figure, we learn, was probably conservative and has since risen to at least 8 percent of all persons required to file.

The GAO study was highly critical of IRS enforcement policies and declared that drastic action is necessary to detect "subterranean income" and to collect the taxes due thereon. Congress must therefore appropriate much greater sums than the $3 billion now allocated to the IRS for its enforcement procedures. The study notes that:

● 52 percent of those with incomes under $5,000 failed to file anything;

● 33 percent of all farm workers were in the same category;

● 64 percent of all private household workers, such as maids and gardeners, failed to file; and

● 17 percent of all non-filers were self-employed. This means that at least 2 million—and probably many more—of the 13 million independent proprietors who make up this principal segment of the middle class simply failed or refused to file any income-tax returns.

The losses to the treasury are staggering, and the IRS simply cannot cope with this number of refusers. It cannot investigate millions who ignore IRS laws and regulations. It costs a fortune to prosecute one rebel . . . what can IRS do with 10 or 20 million?

The IRS seeks by a multitude of press releases to show that the tax rebellion involves only a few people; in one statement it declared that "only 4,500" had filed Fifth Amendment returns last year. This is extremely interesting: ONLY 4,500!

But every one of these, according to IRS pronouncements, has committed a felony or at least a misdemeanor; and how many of them has it indicted, charged, arrested, tried and attempted to convict?

Very, very few indeed. I would say that if a million persons were to file Fifth Amendment returns, the possibility of being tried on the charge of "non-filing" would be about the same as the danger of being struck by a bolt of lightning.

I am absolutely certain of one thing: The day the entire middle class refuses to make returns or pay income taxes—and that can very well happen in the foreseeable future—will be the day on which we can celebrate the demise of the Internal Revenue Service.

# Rebels Winning

We have many times discussed the various devices and arguments used by recalcitrant taxpayers to escape the clutches of the IRS. And we are certain that the war between them is slowly, gradually, but surely being won by the resisters. There are now simply too many of them and they are becoming more and more sophisticated in their methods.

To combat this growing and many-faceted problem, the IRS is constantly inventing new methods of enforcement. For example, in one ploy, it obtained from a private source information concerning people who had not filed any returns in recent years, describing their social status, their apparent living standards and their presumed expenditures for private purposes—the aim being to discover the basis for concluding that these people must have reportable and taxable incomes. Once this information is obtained, telephone calls are made in order to obtain some response and information regarding taxable income. Probing questions are asked in order to elicit information on which charges may be based.

However, any attempt to carry out such a program on a national scale would not only require an enormous amount of preparatory work and expense, but would also, we believe, result in very little success. The targeted citizens could simply refuse to give any information or even to converse with an agent, no matter how many times he called. Or they could state that any communication must be in writing, and letters could be ignored or answered in such a way as to evade any inquiry.

This would leave it strictly up to the IRS to do its own research, which could mean that an impossible amount of time and expense would have to be undertaken; and, if the citizen had taken certain precautions to protect himself, the service would be completely frustrated in its quest for information. If it could not discover any traceable income, it would be left without the means of taking any action, civil or criminal. The family might be living on revenues from tax-exempt securities; there are almost any number of situations in which a man or woman could be living decently and still have no tax liability under IRS law.

## SEARCH FOR SCHEMES

The Associated Press reported in an article datelined May 9, 1984 from Washington, that the IRS was conducting searches in seven cities for evidence of tax evasion schemes.

An instance was cited in which one person had reduced his tax liability by no less than $217,000 simply by making an outlay of $43,000.

The situation is being analyzed to see whether criminal prosecutions can be maintained.

We believe that the promoters of these plans are well able to defend themselves against the IRS and will eventually defeat it.

The problems facing the agency are indeed acute, immense and growing. One recent study placed the unreported underground economy at $600 billion. A recent congressional study officially placed this at $222 billion a year. Sen. Roger W. Jepsen (R-Iowa) declared that it is virtually impossible to make any accurate estimate of its size or extent—since it is so well hidden. But it is quite certain, he added, that "too many Americans continue to conceal their economic activities, primarily to avoid paying taxes."

And what can Congress or the IRS do about this? Very little, indeed. The rebels are winning the war. ●

# *Repeal Passed*

At long last, just before the August 5, 1983 deadline, both houses of Congress finally passed a law repealing the withholding provision on dividends and interest, which had been included—under prodding from President Ronald ·Reagan—in the so-called Tax Equity and Fiscal Responsibility Act of 1982.

You will recall that President John Kennedy attempted to have a similar law passed in 1962. However, the opposition was so strong that the proposal got nowhere.

In 1982-83, similar reactions soon appeared. Members of Congress received several million messages from their constituents condemning the law. The measure was repealed by such an overwhelming majority in both houses that Reagan signed the repeal—although he had previously stated that he would veto it.

The lesson from this is apparent: If enough people bring pressure on Congress, it will obey the popular will—for its members are thinking of the next election. However, we should note that banks, savings and loans and corporations—not knowing what would happen—had spent untold millions of dollars to install the computers necessary if the law went into effect.

However, in order to avoid a veto—or in obedience to the Internal Revenue Service (IRS)—a number of sanctions were suggested.

I can only note suggestions that:

● Taxpayers be required to include their 1090s with their tax returns; and that

● Heavy fines be imposed upon any depositor who declined or refused to give his Social Security (SS) number to any financial institution.

And let us note another rather significant victory for the taxpayers. At one time, almost anyone could establish an "office in the home" and take deductions therefor, if he did any work at all there in connection with his job. Schoolteachers who corrected papers or prepared classwork at home took such deductions. Millions of others who did any such work there did the same.

No doubt, some of these were based on rather inadequate foundations. But then the IRS established extreme rules and regulations, which were far more unjust than any cheating that had been done before. It declared that no one who earned income as an employee could take a deduction for an office in the home.

However, millions of employees work on a contract basis and must maintain offices there or rent commercial space. Furthermore, millions of employees also operate sidelines in their spare time and require office space at home to carry on work totally unrelated to that done as employees. These were all denied deductions for the use of such space and facilities.

Now the IRS admits that all employees working under contract may deduct the rental value of space used as an office in the home. Furthermore, anyone who needs such space in connection with an activity not related to his work as an employee is also entitled to the same privilege.

I have an idea that one reason the IRS has surrendered on this issue is not merely the opposition which arose. I have a notion that a great many "moonlighters"—denied office-space deductions—simply stopped reporting peripheral incomes at all.

As the children used to say when I was a boy, there are more ways than one to skin a cat; and there are various methods by which the IRS may be defeated.

# IRS Personnel in Danger

I well remember my first confrontation with the Internal Revenue Service (IRS). It was in 1946. Upon arriving at its headquarters in Detroit, I was brusquely informed (although I had paid all taxes) that they "knew" that I had evaded $45,000; that they would, before finishing with me, confiscate every dollar I had saved from years of toil and extreme sacrifice; and that they would, in addition, see me behind prison bars. They also forced me to bring all my records to the office and leave them there for 18 months. Finally, I was compelled to prepare the notorious Ten-Year Net Worth Statement.

We have made some progress since then in clipping the IRS agents' claws: They are now very careful not to threaten; they can only **look** at your records once and in the taxpayer's presence; and no agent now dares to demand the Ten-Year Statement.

However, IRS still seizes property without due process of law and constantly violates not only the Constitution but even its own law in various ways against the taxpayers who do not know how to defend themselves.

## ARTILLERY REVERSED

However, angry taxpayers have now reversed the IRS artillery. No longer is it the taxpayers alone who are intimidated—instead it is the agency's personnel. This fact has been revealed from time to time in the news media; and recently an article in the "Wall Street Journal" described further how perilous it is to be an auditing agent when he attempts to collect taxes from frustrated and angry taxpayers.

The physical safety of agents has become a major concern in the service, which now holds regular classes to instruct its personnel in the techniques of personal protection; and the term "PDT's"—"potentially dangerous taxpayers"—has come into common parlance in the service.

"The job of collecting taxes," we read, "has become one of the most dangerous in government. Threats and assaults against IRS agents rose to a record 531 last year, up 14 percent from the year earlier. And in September, 1983, a revenue officer was ambushed and killed in suburban Buffalo, N.Y." (SPOTLIGHT, Oct. 31, 1983, May 32, 1984).

Now some 8,000 front-line agents receive a standard indoctrination on how to calm angry taxpayers and avoid violence.

One teacher of such classes had to live five miles from his place of work; keep an unlisted telephone number; drive an untraceable, rented auto; even so, he was assaulted by a 6-foot-4 tax protester.

During the course, videotapes filled with violence are shown; a farmer is depicted waving a shotgun at an agent and warning him not to return without an army. The agents are told to be firm and calm, but never to threaten or do anything to provoke anger.

Agents are supposed to collect taxes, but they are not expected to risk their lives or their skin. "If you have an account of an illegal tax protester, you had better be wary."

IRS officials declare that more attention must be given to personal safety; and they are demanding increasing benefits, larger salaries and earlier retirement for auditing agents because of the hazardous nature of their occupation. And they are saying that unless such inducements are offered, it will be impossible to recruit competent employees for this work.

# *The Perjury Line*

One man wrote that he had always paid his taxes and made full disclosure; but that now, at the age of 68, he is thoroughly disgusted with the IRS, the federal government in general, and everything related to, or emanating from, them. He stated further that he is now ready to join the Tax Rebellion in anyway he can; and that, as a first step, he plans next year to make full disclosure, pay any tax that may be due, but rub out the perjury line in the 1040 and see what action, if any, the IRS will take thereafter.

Now it so happens that a few years ago I became engrossed in, and intrigued over, the question of the Perjury Line. I wrote to the Commissioner of Internal Revenue asking how perjury could be involved when the return was not sworn to before a notary public. The answer was that no perjury could take place; that the line was merely a "signpost" (or a scarecrow); that the possible penalty for misstatements would be for fraud (three years in prison) instead of five years for perjury.

However, after several communications, the Agency made it plain that the perjury line was absolutely essential for the administration of the IR Code, for without it, no criminal prosecution could be maintained; and the **government would then be able only to bring a civil action based on its own research — a lengthy and difficult procedure with little possibility of profitable results.**

Finally, I asked what the situation would be if a taxpayer made full disclosure, paid all taxes due, and then rubbed out the perjury line. The reply, believe it or not, ran as follows: In that case, the statute of limitations would never begin to run; the return would be regarded as no return at all; the taxpayer could be sent to prison **and fined \$10,000 for failure to file under Section 7203 of the Code; and** even 50 or 100 years later he or his estate could be sued civilly for failure to pay any tax — even after this had been paid in full.

Even the Spanish Inquisition, so far as I know, never attempted to enforce such a rule!

So I apprized my 68-year-old correspondent of the above; and I wrote that I would like to see some individual with a very small tax liability make full disclosure, pay the tax, rub out the perjury line, and then demand a jury trial for criminal violation of Section 7203. Would any jury in the U.S. send a man to prison under these circumstances?

Now consider the potentials: if the IRS cannot enforce criminal sanctions for deleting the perjury line, then it cannot begin a criminal (only a civil) action for any misstatement or omission charged against a taxpayer because of his 1040 return; and this would be the beginning of the end for the Internal Revenue Service in the U.S.

**(Since this article appeared, several taxpayers have written that they have deleted the Perjury Line for years, and the IRS has never taken any criminal or other action against any of them.)**

# *IRS Is Losing*

On April 10, 1984, the "Wall Street Journal" published a long article describing the ongoing conflict—past, present, and probable—between the Internal Revenue Service and the American citizens. The headline declares that the "IRS Is Losing Battle Against Tax Evaders Despite Its New Gear"—i.e., the tools with which it has been provided' to detect resisters and collect the taxes it declares or believes to be due.

The agency attempts to project an image of firmness, fairness and total capacity to deal with every kind of problem and rebellion. However, it does not require much research or knowledge to discover how false this is: "The image is easily shattered," we read.

"The IRS is losing the battle against tax cheats. Its high-tech wizardry and strengthened legal arsenal can't keep pace with an ever-growing army of tax evaders hiding in a jungle of complex laws."

And the author continues with an analysis that is quite similar to what I have been saying for years about the problems that it faces and the various methods used by more and more people to defeat and frustrate our Big Brother on the Potomac in 1984.

The IRS now admits that the tax gap—the amount of lost revenue—has tripled during the last 10 years and now totals at least $100 billion a year. (Actually, there is no doubt that it is far more than that.) Roscoe Egger, IRS commissioner, has admitted that the problem is rapidly growing worse.

The first fact to be noted is that whereas 5 percent of all returns were audited in the 1960s, the number will decline to 1.36 percent this year. Thus, the IRS has neither the competence nor the manpower to employ its most effective weapon against evaders to the extent it would like—and this in spite of the fact that its appropriation has increased from about $2 to some $9 billion or more a year.

It was believed and hoped that the Tax Equity and Fiscal Responsibility Act of 1982 would go a long way toward solving the problem: but the Congress was compelled to repeal withholding on interest and dividends. It is very doubtful that the new provisions will increase voluntary compliance; the IRS is supposed to match all payments shown on 1099s with individual returns—but the fact is that is has not done nor will it do so.

## TOOTHLESS

Time was when the IRS boasted that it was in complete control and it ignored its problems, which had been increasing progressively over the years. But finally, the point was reached that in order to obtain more manpower and much-increased appropriations, it became necessary to publicize the extent of the growing tax revolt and its own incapacity to control it. Thus the image of a toothless tiger has emerged.

Caryl Connor, a former speech-writer for President Jimmy Carter, has been interviewing many hundreds of taxpayers over a three-year period and she declares that almost everyone cheats on federal tax returns. She found only three persons who would declare categorically that they had never done so.

In run-of-the-mill cases, people claimed a dog as a dependent or wrote "M.D." on checks to a cleaning woman and claimed such payments as deductible medical expenses.

However, of far greater importance were larger and more sophisticated schemes. For example, a car salesman bought a junked Cadillac, reported the accident to the police, towed the car back to the junkyard, and took a large casualty loss. An attorney wrote out a check for $10,000 to his college, retrieved $9,000 and reported the larger sum as a charitable contribution (he had his cancelled check to prove it).

Incidentally, I know that many people have used this ploy routinely for years with cooperating charities of various kinds.

Tax shelters, sometimes called "abusive," now constitute one of the greatest and most difficult of IRS headaches. These are now so numerous and complex that the agency must devote a large portion of its resources in attempts to combat them.

Connor declares that the tax code, as now written, is simply impossible to administer. And even tax attorneys, who made huge incomes because of this very fact, are now beginning to admit that drastic simplification (such as advocated in my book "The Great Tax Fraud," written in 1967-68) is the only answer.

## SAFE ENOUGH

However, the article points out a fact which I have emphasized for years—namely, that an independent entrepreneur, if he watches what he does, is absolutely safe in underreporting his income drastically. All he has to do is to deposit no more in banks than he reports and shows on his books; and avoid demonstrable overinvestments during the period covered.

Millions of the self-employed are using this method with complete success. Millions of others in the underground or subterranean economy are receiving their income in cash, keeping little or no money in bank accounts, and reporting nothing at all. This economy has been estimated by experts at more than $500 billion a year.

So the IRS is losing its battle on various fronts and in different ways. After all, it costs perhaps $250,000 to prosecute one tax rebel—and in many cases, they are winning acquittals from informed juries. And whenever the IRS either twists its own laws or applies unjust and un-Constitutional provisions, which destroy completely honest taxpayers, this information seeps into the general public, which, as a result, becomes more and more disillusioned with an agency which has become, as it were, a ravening tiger whenever it can act in that manner and capacity.  ●

# Armed Conflict

In a "manual supplement" dated January 10, 1979, for its employees, the Internal Revenue Service (IRS) declared:

> **Since some illegal tax-protesters advocate violence in dealing with Service personnel, Revenue Officers should attempt to secure payments and returns without personally contacting the protestor outside the office. If personal contact is necessary outside the office, the Revenue Officer should consider being accompanied by an . . . armed escort.**

There you have it! The IRS admits to its own personnel that it has come to an armed conflict with the people.

The extent and the very fact of such violence was long concealed from the general public; but we have now been apprised officially of its existence.

In September, 1980, Alan Stang published an article called "Due Process" in which he told how Don McGrath was shot to death by IRS agents in North Dakota in a dispute over a bill of $39.65.

When the shootout with Gordon Kahl occurred, such violence became national news, and even more so when he was killed in Arkansas.

At any rate, the IRS now officially admits that violence between taxpayers and IRS agents is becoming more frequent and severe. The United Press International, in a syndicated article datelined in Washington, declared that: "Tax-protestors are assaulting Internal Revenue Service agents more frequently; and in one case a contract was put out to kill an IRS employee, IRS Commissioner Roscoe Egger says."

Examples are plentiful: an IRS employee was shot in Cleveland; the types of harassment range from late-night telephone calls to physical threats and actual violence. In 1982, no fewer than 512 verified incidents concerned IRS employees threatened with physical violence or actually attacked—an increase of 60 over the previous year.

Over the past seven years, 3,647 cases of threats or assaults have been investigated by the Security Division of the agency. Egger emphasized in testimony before a Senate subcommittee that while this kind of thing has been going on for years, it has, of late, increased rapidly in frequency and seriousness.

In addition to this, an increasing number of IRS employees are being sued personally for violation of civil rights. Egger demanded that in all cases—no matter what the facts might be—the government itself, i.e. the taxpayers, should be the defendants. He stated that 1,361 civil suits against employees were pending in 1983. Taxpayers and protesters have also filed a multitude of liens against real estate owned by IRS personnel.

The Coeur d'Alene (Idaho) "Press" stated in an article published May 27, 1983, that three taxpayers had filed suits totaling $8 million against seven IRS employees and the father of one of them.

All this is a symptom of the war the federal government is waging, through the IRS, against its own people, who, driven to the extremities of desperation, are reacting as human beings have always done under intolerable stress and extortion.

I predict that the IRS is riding for a great fall; and I can tell you how its collapse could come quickly, certainly, and without even a bloody nose:

(1) Let all employees report enough allowances to eliminate withholding and then make no returns at all; and

(2) Even more decisive and strategic, let all the 25 million self-employed simply stop filing any return for a single year!

That would signal the immediate end and collapse of the IRS!

# Mike Tecton — Tax Crusader

The battle of Mike Tecton of McLean, Va., is, to say the least, unique and instructive. By profession an architect, he had 22 years of experience in designing some 1,000 townhouses and 4,000 single homes, many in the $200,000 to $300,000 class.

He holds 35 patents and had promoted 1,500 products in the commercial and industrial fields. He has written more than a dozen books and pamphlets and has contributed extensively to newspapers and other publications and, of late, has appeared on several hundred radio and TV programs.

For about 12 or 13 years, while making from $25,000 to $40,000 a year, he filed no income-tax returns and was left undisturbed by the IRS. We have little doubt that had he continued as a silent and unobtrusive rebel, he, like millions of others, would have been left undisturbed by the IRS to keep and enjoy the money he earned.

However, this was not to be: for late in 1973, he experienced a volcanic implosion which, by its emotional impact, transformed him into a crusader against the present form of federal taxation, with a conviction so profound that he was willing to risk everything on the issue.

Tecton determined, as a result of studying the Constitution, that the Internal Revenue Code is designed to create classes or castes in American society and to deprive our citizens of the rights guaranteed under the Constitution. Actually, it establishes an elite nobility, on the one hand, because of its loopholes; and, on the other, a vast class of tax-slaves, doomed to support them.

Again and again Tecton emphasized that he was not fighting taxation — only unequal taxation.

On June 16, he was arraigned in the U.S. District Court of Alexandria, Va., on the charge of failing to file income tax returns for 1971, 1972, and 1973; and the next day he appeared on the steps of the Capitol in Washington carrying a huge sign proclaiming "Tax Equality" and burning a 1040 form.

Tecton's trial in September, 1974, resulted in a 10 to 2 deadlock in which all those who voted to convict him were government employees. On Oct. 22, he was tried again and this time convicted. He states that he was never indicted by a grand jury; that the judge told him he would be held in contempt if he mentioned to the jury that he had already been tried on the same offense, that the court refused to permit him to put a single witness on the stand; that his request to keep federal employees off the jury was denied; that the judge threatened him with contempt if he even mentioned the Constitution; that federal employees in the next room made such a racket that the jury could not hear what he said; that the judge tried to have him sentenced to 90 days in jail for calling his suppression of evidence unfair.

Nevertheless, he was only sentenced to pay a fine of $300 and undergo six months of unsupervised probation; he attributes this light sentence to his favorable press coverage and the fact that he sued everyone concerned with his trial and conviction for depriving him of his civil rights. (Now, the government is trying to jail Tecton for "violation" of his "unsupervised probation.")

Tecton declares that he has just begun to fight and that he wants to help all other tax-rebels everywhere in the nation.

# The Underground Economy

We have discussed certain phases of the intensifying tax revolt, together with official admissions of impotence by the IRS to deal with it and the frustrations of its agents trying to combat it. Now let us consider various other important sources of information.

While one government official admitted that at least $135 billion of income—not even including that of non-filers—was going untaxed, we find that other authorities believe the true losses to be far greater.

Prof. Peter M. Gutman, for example, of the College of the City University of New York, stated in an article published in "Business World" (March 13, 1978), that the underground economy alone had already reached at least $195 billion in 1977. This did not include losses from underreporting, barter and exchange, and other forms of tax avoidance and evasion. Various other investigators placed the losses at much greater totals, in one case $521 billion.

On April 10, 1979, Mary Jo Messner published an article in the Philadelphia "Daily News" in which she stated that barter and exchange—some tax-exempt but much taxable according to IRS regulations—totals not less than $15 billion. A trade of like for like—as one ball player for another—is tax-exempt, as is a carpenter job for one of plumbing or one apartment building for another.

However, if an automobile is exchanged for something of an intangible nature—such as a bond—or a professional service, then tax-exemption does not apply. Nevertheless, many a farmer, for example, will trade vegetables for dental care and report no taxable event or income. What can the IRS do about it anyway, unless the transaction is reported?

An article in the "Daily Oklahoman" (May 29, 1979) reported that although the IRS had definitely identified 1.6 million "tax-cheaters" in 1978, it was able to try and convict only a total of 247.

Patrick Wright, in an article published July 19, 1979, in the "Monthly Detroit," declared that waiters at two restaurants lug home $60,000 in tips, little of which is reported for income taxation. He stated also that 15,000 prostitutes ply their trade in the Motor City with average annual incomes of $30,000 on which they pay no income taxes—revenues which add up to $450 million a year. (We should note that under the "Garner" decision, these women are not even required to file returns since their income derives from illicit sources.)

A great many other similar articles are included in a 236-page document published by the House Subcommittee on Government Operations. However, we consider the one appearing in "U.S. News & World Report" (Oct. 22, 1979) the most interesting and revealing. It estimates that the underground economy alone now involves between 15 and 20 million individuals who fail to report incomes totaling not less than $500 billion.

The author declares that at least 4.5 million persons derive their entire income from such activity, while the remainder moonlight, and forget to report all income therefrom. He describes various methods by which unreported income is obtained. A 24-year-old actress in New York works as a bartender for $30 or $35 a week; she helps out in her father's jewelry store; and she performs occasionally in a cabaret at a Greenwich Village night spot.

Techniques are legion:

● A great many take in boarders or rent a room or two or an apartment;

● One woman makes a career of weekly garage sales;

● Another earns $200 a week by sewing children's clothing;

● Farmers operate roadside vegetable and fruit stands;

● A musician earns $8,000 a year giving guitar lessons;

● An employee of a large garage has his own shop at home where he makes repairs at much lower prices;

● Thousands, perhaps millions, conduct door-to-door sales of various kinds of merchandise;

● Taxi drivers pocket half or more of their income;

● Barbers and beauty-shop operators keep their reported income below taxation levels, or report nothing at all;

● A self-employed illustrator works at home and reports no income;

● Many collect unemployment benefits while earning many kinds of unreported income;

● Some with low or no other income, collect the bets at racetracks for high winners;

● A plasterer will do jobs at substantial reductions for payments in cash.

But why continue? The methods and techniques of tax evasion are without number and limited only by the ingenuity of perpetrators.

I say the IRS has its hands full. What do you think?

# Fighting Tyranny

Lucille Moran was one of the most outstanding of the fighters against IRS tyranny in the United States; it has been said that she caused the agency more trouble and loss of revenue than anyone else.

From her headquarters in Tavernier, Florida, she disseminated a constant stream of literature, such as her "How to Refuse Income Taxes Legally" and "Taxation Depends on Confession."

She declared that no one can be compelled to file a 1040 and that almost all indictments, assessments and convictions obtained against taxpayers are based on information which they themselves supply. She pointed out again and again that by filing a return under "penalties of perjury," the taxpayer waives all his Constitutional rights.

If he is guilty of any misstatement or omission, he commits a felony, punishable by long prison terms and heavy fines. A mere failure to file, however, is only a misdemeanor which millions are now committing with complete immunity.

**NO CHECKS, PLEASE**

She refused to accept personal checks from her clients since those would leave a paper trail which the IRS could investigate as a basis for prosecution of everyone concerned. She took a strong stand against the use of the Fifth Amendment return or any other indicating protest; for these are like red flags waved in the face of a bull.

But when people simply drop out of the system, nothing is fed into the computers, and, in due course, the IRS becomes helpless to attack. This, she reiterated, is the only effective method by which to defeat the monster which seeks total control over our lives and finances.

Commenting on Sec. 7203—which makes the failure to file the "confession sheet" a crime—she observed that a good informer is worth 50 FBI agents. Also, she noted that if crooks and hoods would only cooperate by sending in annual reports concerning their activities to their friendly neighborhood FBI offices, federal agents could enjoy the fun of busting them for their crimes. Such shady characters could then be prosecuted and convicted for failure to supply information, and the culprits could be sent to prison at little cost.

But the criminals know their rights. They will not give testimony against themselves or against anyone else unless they receive guarantees of immunity. It is only the decent, honest, hard-working citizen whom the government punishes by forcing him to make a complete disclosure of all his business and activity. He submits because he does not know his rights.

**DROP OUT**

Filing nothing whatever and then disappearing from sight is the technique Miss Moran advocated. Give the computers no data and they will have nothing with which to work. When the IRS fails to receive a return, it sends three or four form letters demanding compliance.

But it admits that it is able to contact only a comparatively small fraction of the dropouts, and even when it does so the collection of taxes is extremely difficult and often impossible.

When there is no response or contact, the computers become helpless and then there are no more letters.

Miss Moran noted that in 1977 in Florida alone, 300,000 citizens failed to file any return. Extrapolate this for the whole country, and you have at least 10 million for that date—a number which has probably at least doubled since then. How, she demanded, can the IRS contend with all these dropouts, when it can audit only a small fraction of the people who file various types of protest returns as well as highly questionable conventional ones—including the millions of self-employed who admittedly under-report their taxable incomes by at least 40 percent?

That her technique has been highly effective is an established fact. The "Wall Street Journal" noted in an article published March 20, 1980, that her clients were found in every state and constituted one of the most important elements in the tax protest movement.

**CHARGE DROPPED**

However, what I had long expected finally happened when Miss Moran was indicted by a grand jury for "aiding and abetting" in the preparation of fraudulent income tax returns.

I wrote her that the charge was ridiculous, since she never aided or abetted in the preparation of any return, but simply told people not to file anything at all. Ironically, there is no law forbidding this practice.

After the government employed 47 special agents who investigated her contacts in some 23 states in its preparation for a criminal trial, all charges were suddenly dropped. So she remained free and completely triumphant.

On July 5, 1983, I received a telephone call from one of her friends that she had passed away in her sleep during the previous night.

Thus, this gallant lady rests in peace after a very vigorous and turbulent career, the effects of which will stretch far into the future. •

# Fourth Amendment Defense

The victory of Dr. Vincent R. Hill, a medical practitioner in Illinois, who refused to surrender his records to the IRS, is another landmark in the battle of American citizens against the Washington monster.

After obtaining a court warrant to seize them, the agency entered the doctor's office and home and carried away a truckload of his papers and records, thinking that the action was legal under the Fourth Amendment.

However, the doctor carried his battle to the Seventh Circuit Court of Appeals, which, on May 17, 1971, declared the seizure illegal, since the warrant did not describe precisely what was to be taken and since it was not obtained under oath or affirmation.

**The higher court therefore decreed that the material must be returned and that no information obtained from it could be used in any civil or criminal proceeding.**

Thus, once and for all it was established, that even a warrant is not sufficient authority to seize private papers unless the proceeding meets all constitutional requirements.

It is interesting to note that the IRS did not appeal the Hill decision to the Supreme Court, since it well knew that its defeat there would be even more decisive and final.

These Circuit Court determinations are now so well known that even the IRS cannot ignore them. However, IRS routinely ignores other U.S. District Court decisions which it does not like and which it hopes will not be known by the taxpayers.

# *Battle Plan*

Peggy Christensen (SPOTLIGHT, Aug. 29) cautions prospective litigants with the Internal Revenue Service (IRS) not to write anything that might later be used to prejudice a jury against them. They should always be respectful. They should declare their love for their country and their veneration for the Constitution. And they should offer to file any desired document if an explanation will be given how this can be done without waiving Constitutional rights. Since no answer has ever been given to this question, it is a powerful opening move.

She then offers a model letter to be written in reply to an IRS statement that no return, or no satisfactory return, has been received. Here she summarizes the Bill of Rights and shows how several of its provisions are routinely violated by the service.

The letter declares: "We are taking the Fifth Amendment, not because we have done anything wrong. On the contrary, we are claiming rights that so many men and women have bled and died to attain, to protect them from being violated by those who would take away our freedom, through taxes or any other means."

She then cites various court decisions on which the citizen may rely in justifying the actions he has taken.

In another model letter, the citizen asks the district director of the IRS whether any information in a return could be used in a criminal prosecution. And passages are cited from "Garner" and other Supreme Court decisions.

The second portion of "Peggy's Book" (SPOTLIGHT, Aug. 22) explains how to protect bank records and other private documents by using the Privacy and Freedom of Information acts. The latter is reprinted in full, together with instructions concerning its use.

One of the most significant portions of the book consists of suggested pre-trial motions, which the defense may offer.

Motions to achieve the following are included. To:

● Dismiss because of lack of probable cause;

● Inspect and copy records, papers and other relevant materials;

● Enlarge time to file pre-trial motions;

● Continue and waive speedy trial because of difficulty in obtaining competent and affordable counsel;

● Discuss indictment based upon the Fifth Amendment "privilege" and the Privacy Act;

● Disclose grand jury minutes, testimony and informants;

● Disclose any and all surveillance, eavesdropping or observance;

● Exclude employees of the plaintiff or their relatives from jury duty and to permit a *voir dire* by the defense; and

● Disclose any inducements, promises or payments the government made to prospective witnesses.

Following this, we have an analysis of the trial itself. And here we find a unique element of defense. When a person declares himself "exempt" on the W-4 Form, he must state that he incurred no "tax liability" the previous year and does not expect to incur one during the present.

The point is that nowhere in the IR Code is tax liability defined—as is also the case with "income." And since "experts" who have worked in the IRS for many years cannot define either income or tax liability, how can a simple working man be expected to know what either one is?

A person who has invoked the Fifth Amendment should simply declare that he believes in the Constitution. But since no one in the IRS has been able to explain to him how to fill out a 1040 under penalties of perjury without waiving his Constitutional rights, he simply used a privilege available to everyone without the possibility of committing a crime willfully.

The most significant of the suggested *voir dire* questions to be submitted to members of the jury run as follows:

● Are you now or have you ever been an employee of the Internal Revenue Service of the federal government?

● Do you presently receive Social Security or any form of welfare from the government?

● Is your spouse or any close relative employed by the IRS or any other government agency?

● Have you any opinion concerning the guilt or innocence of the defendant in this case?

● If the majority of the jurors were to believe the accused guilty and you did not, would you permit the majority to influence you for any reason?

The final section deals with instructions to be given to the jury by the court at the close of the trial. Since it is of the utmost importance that these include every valid statement and all dicta based upon Supreme Court decisions that could influence the jury to acquit, Peggy has prepared a list of 27 proposals that should be included in such instructions. Among these are:

● Assertions of the Fifth Amendment rights;

● Right to make good-faith challenges;

● Nature of willfulness;

● Meaning of intent vs motive;

● Waiver of Constitutional rights by filing a 1040;

● Fifth Amendment provides protection for the innocent as well as for the guilty against self-incrimination;

● U.S. Constitution is the supreme law of the land;

● Burden of proof is on the government;

● Verdict must represent the considered conscience of every member of the jury;

● IR code is too ambiguous, complicated and confusing to be understood by ordinary citizens;

● Specific intent of willfulness must be established beyond a reasonable doubt in order to secure a conviction;

● Legal meaning of willfulness;

● If no tax has been assessed, taxpayer has no tax liability;

● Since tax liability is nowhere defined in the IR code, it can be established only by taxpayer admission, by agreement with the IRS or by a court of competent jurisdiction; and finally

● Even if you find substantial evidence of tax violation, you must consider the issue of selective or discriminatory prosecution in this case.

As we noted before, Peggy has assisted in 65 cases, which have resulted in jury acquittals. She has available, at $25 each, the transcripts of 15 such victories.

The material supplied by Peggy Christensen embodies an education in itself. And I suggest that those who wish to learn more of it may write her in care of the Golden Mean Society, PO Box 7733, Missoula, Montana 59807.

# Jerome Daly — Long Time Tax Rebel

Perhaps the toughest, hardiest, and most inveterate of all the tax rebels is Jerome Daly of Minnesota, who once told this writer that, since he was born in a corn-crib, no hardship could faze him.

He first made history in 1968 when the First National Bank of Montgomery, Minn., attempted to seize his home because he was delinquent in mortgage payments.

At a jury trial in Credit River Township, he was awarded the property, debt-free, because he demonstrated that since the bank had not given him anything of value when it created credit out of nothing on its books, it was not entitled to seize his real estate. The bank did not appeal.

However, a much greater battle was to come. Beginning for the year 1965, Daly filed his income tax return in blank, with an attachment explaining that Federal Reserve notes did not qualify as constitutional money or legal tender and therefore did not constitute dollar income within the meaning of the Internal Revenue Code.

When Daly was ordered by U.S. District Judge Miles Lord to appear at the IRS office on January 6, 1967, he did so. But Daly refused to be sworn, answer questions or produce records. On March 27, the judge sentenced him to prison for contempt of court. Daly appealed.

On April 11, 1968, a panel of three U.S. judges for the Eighth Circuit Court remanded the case for a plenary trial, where, on July 17, an epoch-making event occurred.

For the first time, it was established that all provisions in the Internal Revenue Code (and there are many of them) which make it a crime not to answer questions, keep records, or surrender the same, are null and void. Daly won a complete and devastating victory.

However, the IRS was not through with Daly. It took them nearly four years to bring criminal charges against him for failing to file. He was convicted on Oct. 14, 1972.

Although his case was on appeal, he was arrested and sent to the Springfield, Mo., Medical Center on Oct. 22, 1973, where his stamina and public support were so great that he was soon released on probation, with the restriction that he he was not to leave Minnesota without permission.

However, since he paid no attention to this, he was arrested in Pennsylvania early in 1974 and sent to the federal facility at Sandstone, Minn., where he served about eight months.

**(NOTE: Later, Daly organized the Basic Bible Church with its affiliate, the Order of Almighty God [similar in some respects to apostolic orders in the Catholic Church], whose members divested themselves of property and conveyed their personal incomes to the Order.**

**(For this, he incurred the wrath of the IRS. After a four-month trial in Texas, which cost the government more than $1 million, and in which he was accused of mail fraud, he was convicted, sentenced to 16 years in prison, and fined $92,000. We understand that as of December, 1984 he is at the Lompoc federal facility in California.)**

# Charles Riely: Victorious Rebel

Charles Riely, a resident of Mesa, Arizona, is another outstanding figure in the national tax resistance movement. For years, he operated the Tri-City Printing Co., a successful enterprise, which produced such material as *The Big Bluff,* authored by Marvin Cooley. He called attention to himself by conducting weekly meetings under the auspices of the Caucus Club and, as the years went by, became more and more active in the work.

We presume it inevitable that sooner or later the IRS would move to punish and silence this outspoken rebel. However, even the preliminaries in this prosecution proved expensive and time-consuming for the government.

One of its early maneuvers was to obtain all his bank records in order to establish reportable or taxable income. However, by using the protections available under Sec. 7609 of the IR Code, Mr. Riely was able to postpone a final decision concerning the matter by the Ninth Circuit Court of Appeals for nearly three years. When the IRS was finally told that it must pay the bank several hundred dollars to cover the cost of finding and duplicating the records, the Agency decided to get along without them.

Finally the IRS secured a grand jury indictment, and a three-day trial was held in the U.S. District Court in Phoenix, Arizona, in 1978. This proved to be one of the most significant in the tax resistance movement. Mr. Riely was represented by two young attorneys, McClelland and McPherson, who compiled an enviable record in due course defending similar cases, in several of which they won acquittals and in others very light sentences.

Mr. Riely's was a straight Fifth-Amendment defense. He declared that he could not make a full disclosure without exposing himself to the danger of possible self-incrimination. He used the **Garner** and similar defenses to the utmost; he would not—nor could he be required to—reveal the elements which might lead to prosecution for he alone could know and evaluate these.

The jury acquitted him on all three counts; and he experienced an exhilaration which is difficult for anyone to understand who has not been subjected to a similar ordeal.

Mr. Riely at once emerged not only as a national proponent of the tax resistance movement but as one who spoke in accents of confidence and triumph. He has been conducting meetings and seminars around the country in which large audiences learn his methods and techniques.

Shortly after his victory, Mr. Riely sold his printing establishment and devoted himself exclusively to the movement. He now operates what he calls the Golden Mean Society and conducts a very extensive bookselling business in which he offers a great many titles for sale through mail orders.*

We understand that previous to his indictment and trial, he created an irrevocable trust which has placed his possessions legally beyond the possibility of seizure by the government or anyone else.

The future will reveal what if anything, the IRS can do to silence or injure this outspoken and successful rebel.

*For information, contact **Charles Riely, Box 60, Mesa, Ariz. 85201; (602) 833-1455.**

# Marvin Cooley: Orator and Symbol

Perhaps no one else involved in the tax resistance movement has appealed to the American imagination as has Marvin Cooley, a one-time Mesa, Arizona, farmer, a member of the Mormon Church, once an organizer for the John Birch Society.

After he published *The Big Bluff* in 1972, held seminars in many cities, and appeared on various radio and TV programs, he was indicted and tried—not for tax evasion—but on charges of filing improper returns for 1968, 1969 and 1970. The fact is that he could probably have filed conventional returns without tax liability, since he had a large family; but his opposition was based on principle, not personal considerations.

After three days of testimony, the jury returned a guilty verdict on April 30, 1973. Since the government was determined to make an example of Marvin, it showed no mercy. He was sentenced to and served the maximum term in prison, and also denied bail. Further, he had to pay $6,500 of non-refundable fines in order to avoid immediate incarceration. We understand that he was offered probation if he would agree to discontinue his crusade and make ordinary income tax returns in the future—conditions which he spurned with scorn.

He went to prison in 1974. When he was released in 1976, he was given a magnificent banquet, attended by hundreds of admirers.

In his returns for 1968-70, he wrote "I don't know" on lines where income was to be shown. He declared that he had none that was reportable because Federal Reserve notes are not dollars nor are they constitutional money.

However, after his release, he began using the Fifth Amendment defense exclusively. And, unlike some others, such as Jim Scott of Fresno, California, he did not fade from sight, but became more active than ever. In fact, he emerged as the symbol of the tax resistance movement. He writes for various papers; conducts seminars constantly; files Fifth Amendment returns; and publishes a monthly newsletter, *Tuff Talk*, focusing on legal taxpayer protections.

In an exclusive interview featured in the magazine section of the Arizona *Republic* on January 21, 1979, he explained his technique in detail. The Fifth Amendment, he declared, is his only defense and the only one which can be used successfully by tax resisters; the money issue and others sometimes used can lead only to losses and convictions.

In addition to *The Big Bluff*, which has gone through many printings, he has published a number of other books, among which are *Tea Party, 1976* and *The Patriot's Fighting Packet*.

In his monthly newsletter, *Tuff Talk*, he gives the names of persons who, under his guidance, have used his techniques of defense successfully. He supplies materials for a reasonable fee, which can be used by those who follow his advice and suggestions.*

Although the IRS certainly is well aware that Mr. Cooley has a substantial income from seminars and publications, it has not, to our knowledge, lifted a finger during recent years to interfere with his activities or to bring any further charges against him. In this, he is following, at least to some degree, the course first used by Austin Flett, who said that if you want to fight the IRS, don't have any seizable property or any traceable income. The future will tell what the government can do, if anything, to silence this perennial and outspoken rebel patriot.

*For information, contact Marvin Cooley, 525 E. Baseline Road, Mesa, Ariz. 85204; (602) 892-0569.

# Ch. 2

# Why the Middle Class Rebellion?

# Producers Expand

One of the most extraordinary developments on the American scene during the last 30 years has been the expansion of the "middle class."

Such persons are never employees; and, in most cases, they are not employers either. They run their own businesses, keep their own books, make their own reports, pay their own taxes. They are self-reliant and want a strictly limited government.

Most important of all, they must make their own economic decisions. And since they cannot prosper or even survive in business if they make too many errors, they tend to think for themselves in the political sphere also. For these reasons, they are anathema to communists, socialists and all central bureaucracies of every kind, which seek always to regiment and control all members of society.

### PROPRIETORS DESTROYED

The independents doing business with the public are known in the Internal Revenue Service as "proprietors." In 1946, there were only 5.6 million of them in the United States, for, during World War II, the Franklin Roosevelt administration had destroyed hundreds of thousands of them.

However, by 1979, there were more than 12 million, and now at least 13 million.

In addition to these, many others belong in the same general category:

- 3 million farmers;
- 6 million consultants or salesmen working on contract or for commissions;
- At least half a million professionals; and
- Several million landlords, most of the smaller variety.

Altogether, these constitute an army of nearly 25 million units, who, with their spouses and grown children, could, if organized and educated into a great voting bloc, gain control of the federal and most state governments.

Now what is the secret of this extraordinary development? Well, I would say it is precisely what sustained me after I established a paint store in 1935, when money was so scarce that it had almost disappeared.

How could I, who then knew nothing about paint, wallpaper or a retail business, succeed against such overwhelming odds?

### INCENTIVE

I'll tell you how. It was because of incentive and motivation. I worked 12 hours a day. And it was years before I was able to lay aside any substantial amount of money. I worked 12,000 hours before I had any surplus. I lived on $1 a day, in a small room, at the back of my store.

My objective was to achieve economic independence. In 15 years, I retired with a competence sufficient to maintain me in some degree of comfort and security for the rest of my life.

A similar incentive or motivation activates the millions of proprietors whose reported gross income increased from $79 billion in 1946 to $443 billion in 1979—in spite of considerable under-reporting. If we add to this the income of farmers, salesmen, consultants, professionals and landlords, I have no doubt that it would total at least $1 trillion.

To me, the most important factor involved in all this is the fact that these are the people who believe in the kind of limited government created by our Founding Fathers.

Let us do everything in our power to inform, protect and advance the interest of these people, who have made America the best country in the world and who can make it even better by ridding this nation of the ulcers and excrescences that have grown within and upon our body politic.

●

# IRS vs. the Middle Class

We have been discussing the traps and snares in the IRS Code, and how important it is to avoid them. Now I wish to cover another facet of the great war that goes on constantly between the IRS and taxpayers—especially the free-enterprise, middle class sector of society.

We should understand that every bureaucracy hates and fears an independent middle class for various reasons:

● Because its members seek no favors from the government, they cannot be bribed.

● Since their incomes cannot be determined easily or accurately, they cannot be policed in the manner dear to the heart of every bureaucrat.

● Even more important: since they must make independent and correct decisions in order to prosper or even to survive economically, they also tend to think independently in the political sphere.

Since the federal government has become a vast system of extortion and bribery and since the business independents—of whom there are about 20 million—lie beyond the bounds of such bribery, the IRS has redoubled its extortionary efforts in regard to them in order to accomplish, so far as possible, their destruction or at least their repression.

Thus, in addition to using the traps in the code to injure them, the IRS operates by pure bluff on a very extensive scale. The code is so complicated that no one can understand it fully. It has been said that clever IRS agents can find something in 99 per cent of all returns on which to hang an additional assessment; and this is done in literally hundreds of thousands of cases every year.

Remember that unless an agent can produce at least $100 for every hour he spends with a taxpayer, his efforts are counter-productive. The measure of his success consists in the number and ratio of quick consent-assessments he is able to obtain from taxpayers, who often pay substantial sums rather than spend the time or money necessary to defend themselves. This has given rise to a vicious quota system which, though denied, certainly exists in one form or another.

There is no doubt that in the majority of these cases, much less would be paid if the taxpayers offered a determined and intelligent defense; and in countless instances, they would pay nothing at all.

The principal purpose of my manual, "How to Defend Yourself Against the IRS," is precisely to enable taxpayers to protect themselves from government rapacity and dishonesty, and to do it without the aid of a CPA or attorney.

They will learn how to force IRS agents to cite the exact authorities on which they base assessments; how to go to the Appellate level, where disputes are nominally settled at 40 cents on the dollar and even to the Tax Court, where they are adjudicated at 30 cents; and in countless cases for nothing at all.

If several million taxpayers would follow the advice and techniques offered in my manual, IRS operations would soon become impossible.

It is therefore my hope that a considerable portion of all SPOTLIGHT readers will take advantage of this possibility and thus help to bring about an early termination of the most flagrant violation of the Constitution that has ever existed in this country.

It boasts of Thomas Jefferson as a Founding Father, but he would turn over in his grave if he could know what has been going on in Washington.

# *Middle Class Tax Burdens*

Before me lies a typical newspaper article intended to justify the federal income tax system. It states that "On the whole, the tax burden falls fairly proportionately on middle and upper-income groups.

"Families in the top 20 per cent of income pay 60 per cent of all taxes and, for all the publicity given to those high-income taxpayers who pay no income tax, they represent only two-thirds of one percent of all high-income taxpayers."

Then, however, we have a correct and contradictory statement which demolishes the entire position of the article: "The average family of four with an income of $14,000 pays 22.7 per cent of its income in direct taxes alone." The really high-income groups probably average less than five per cent of their actual (not their reported) income.

The article then declares that our system does not make the rich richer and the poor poorer; largely because those in the upper-income group do pay heavy taxes and the poor receive enormous subsidies—the latter statement being true, for those in the middle incomes finance the bureaucracy and its gratuities to those who do not work.

The apologist misses the real point. What we have said all along is that the middle-income group—those earning from about $8,000 to about $35,000—bear the brunt of all taxation, whether it be income, property, use or sales.

What the writer ignores is that while only a few in the high brackets pay no tax, those who pay only a small percentage even of reported income constitute the great majority among the very wealthy. In the first place, they have at their disposal a multitude of tax-shelters which drastically reduce or eliminate entirely the necessity of paying taxes; and there are 27 categories of income listed in the Code (Sections 101-127) which are not even includable in gross income, which means that they are never reported at all. One of these is income from tax-exempt bonds, which now total about $1 trillion and produce about $50 billion of revenue annually, almost all of it received by those in the high-income brackets.

And so the apologists for those who profit by a tax system based on inequity and injustice continue to fulminate their distortions. But the people are learning and are no longer so easily deceived as once they were.

The people are trying as best they can to strike back; as we pointed out a couple of weeks ago, the millions of independents have now joined the tax rebellion in their own way. If people have to become crooks and liars in order to survive, they will become crooks and liars.

I remember once hearing a philosopher of sorts explain that the difference between big people and little people is that the former steal big things like railroads while the little people steal little things, like apples. The European share cropping peasantry used to go out at night into the potato patches and dig up a few tubers so that a meal could be prepared to feed their famished children.

I think it was Francis Bacon, the Lord Verulam, who declared in one of his Essays that the ways to gain riches are legion, and most of them wicked. Well, he should have known: for when he, as a judge, was charged with corruption, his defense was that, since he took bribes from both sides in the cases he was hearing, the course of justice was not disturbed.

# *Small Business Rebels*

The New York "Times" published an extremely interesting and informative article (reprinted in the Arizona "Republic" on August 7, 1977) which states that a "special research program of the Internal Revenue Service has disclosed that the willingness of small businesses to pay their taxes has slipped to dismally low levels."

Our research has established beyond doubt that millions of small and medium entrepreneurs are now deeply involved in the tax rebellion either by refusing to make any reports at all to the IRS or—what is more prevalent—drastically understating their taxable income.

And, since there are now at least 13 million such independents, their sheer number and the impossibility of reconstructng their incomes by the IRS, makes it absolutely impossible for the service to cope with the problem.

Even though the IRS has filled its code with traps and snares intended to destroy the independent businessman, these cannot in any way combat a situation in which a business is able to display well-kept records, which, however, probably admit only about 80 or 85 per cent of actual gross income, which means that net or taxable income is understated by perhaps more than 50 per cent.

The IRS is well aware of this situation, but is powerless to bring either civil or criminal action against careful and experienced manipulators of their own books and income.

"This recalcitrance," continues the New York "Times," "is costing the government billions of dollars . . ." Indeed it is; and I have estimated that this evasion is saving these middle-class independents and costing the Treasury perhaps not less than $100 billion a year.

We recall that Benjamin Franklin is reported to have said at the Constitutional Convention in 1788 that if a federal income tax were enacted, it would transform almost our entire population into crooks and liars; and it seems to us that the federal government, through the IRS, is doing its utmost to accomplish precisely this result.

The average individual, human nature being what it is, would much rather survive through dishonesty than be destroyed by his own honesty.

The IRS, we are told, states that large corporations and employees are paying 90 per cent of their tax bills: i.e., their cheating totals only 10 per cent. However, when we realize that the IRS collects more than $150 billion from these two sources, we have an underpayment of at least $15 billion. But listen to what else the IRS has to say: in 1965, compliance among small businesses was 78 per cent; in 1969, 69 per cent; but in 1974, only 53 per cent!

Although there is no estimate of how great the dollar loss is because of this "non-compliance," we can make some fairly accurate estimates. Let us say that 13 million small businesses have average gross incomes of $100,000: this would total $1,300 billion. If the understatement of income averages 20 per cent, this would be $260 billion; and, since a 20 per cent understatement of gross means at least a 50 per cent understatement of net, this would be at least $130 billion.

If the average tax on this, if reported, would be 40 per cent, we have an admitted minimum tax loss of $50 billion. There is no doubt that the true amount is considerably greater.

Thus, the IRS officially declared that its tax losses, because of outright evasion, were at least $65 billion. We have no doubt that the actual amount in 1984 is not less than $125 billion.

# Independents in Open Rebellion

We know—and the IRS knows—that many business independents who keep their own books and are known as proprietors, who make their own reports to the taxing authorities and pay only the taxes required on such reported income, have, over the years, been under-reporting their gross and net incomes. And so long as books are kept in good condition and bank accounts are in agreement, the IRS is virtually helpless to do anything about this sort of thing, which has now, in order to make economic survival possible, become almost universal.

In 1972, according to the 1975 "Statistical Abstract," pp. 490-1, 10,173,000 proprietorships had gross receipts of $275.994 billion and net profits of $39.113 billion in the U.S., which averages out at $3,840 of taxable income for each one. The IRS knows that the underreporting of net must average about 50 percent. No doubt this illegal activity is now reducing Treasury income by some $30 or $40 billion a year.

This practice is not only widespread, but perpetrated openly. A Chicago publication, "People & Taxes," in its February, 1978, issue, states that in addition to loopholes for the rich and tax-writeoffs as business expenses, outright lying has now become almost universal among those who handle their own finances—which is the case with all the self-employed, who now make up at least 20 million taxpaying units. In fact, it includes practically all those whose incomes do not derive from wages, salaries, or commissions.

The Chicago "Sun-Times" published a series of articles examining this phenomenon in depth; and it concluded that "a substantial portion of our supposedly respectable fellow citizens are nothing better than common thieves..." The biggest ripoff consists in "the common small business practice of understating receipts by a standard percentage on the books for tax purposes."

One bar owner boasted: "I've got a bookkeeper who knows the score. I'm making $1,400 a week and reporting $400. That means $4,000 to $5,000 a month tax free. Listen, when I started in this business, I was broke. Now I got half a million. I make 30 to 40 grand a year. If you looked at my tax returns, you'd think I was on food stamps."

The normal procedure is to keep two sets of books—one showing only 60 percent of the gross as income. Accounting firms which specialize in this field sometimes re-create the phony accounts from correct ones supplied by the businessman. When one tavern-keeper consulted 10 tax accountants, all but two recommended fraud by skimming off the top, keeping two sets of books, and thus underreporting the net-taxable income anywhere from 20 to 70 percent.

The IRS has declared officially that the "compliance level" among small businesses is 52.6 percent—that is, they underreport net income by 47.4 percent.

I believe it was Benjamin Franklin who declared at the Constitutional Convention in Philadelphia in 1775 that an income tax would transform the government into despotism and the taxpayers into cheats and criminals.

# Middle Class Growth and Power

The middle class, as I define it, consists of individuals who invest both labor and capital in their own economic activity, and derive their livelihood therefrom. They are never employees, and in most cases, have no employees.

They keep their own books and records, and offer their services or goods to the public in competition with large corporations.

They ask nothing from government except protection against violence and other crime. Consequently they resent interference from government in their daily lives and voluntarily accept only reasonable taxation.

Since they must make correct economic decisions in order to prosper or even survive, they tend also to think independently in the political sphere.

Since their incomes cannot be determined accurately by the IRS, this agency hates the independent proprietors and seeks by all possible methods to harass, injure, impoverish or destroy them. Since the middle class constitute the backbone of representative and republican government, every kind of autocracy and despotism seeks their elimination, whether it be a landed aristocracy, a clerical hierarchy, a socialist or communist regime, a financial oligarchy or any other centralized bureaucracy.

The same is true of the great labor bosses, since they cannot control or collect dues from private entrepreneurs and since the middle class reduces the number of those employed by corporations and therefore under the thumb of union officials.

The reason communist or socialist revolutions have occurred in such countries as Russia, Poland, Italy, China, Portugal, Spain, the Balkan states etc, was that in them no well-developed middle class had come into existence, one strong enough to lead a movement to establish a republican state.

Our Founding Fathers could create a truly republican government and give us the Constitution and its Bill of Rights because here the majority of the population were members of a class who earned their living by operating their own freeholds.

It is interesting, informative and heartening to note that, in spite of every effort by the federal government to injure or destroy the middle class, the number of proprietors increased from 5.6 million in 1945 to 13 million in 1980; and the gross income of the class increased from $79 billion to an estimated $1 trillion or even more. In addition to business proprietors (persons specifically in business for themselves, offering goods and services to the public) there are about 3 million farmers; 600,000 professionals; 6 million salesmen and consultants and 6 million landlords (who, in most cases, have other incomes as employees, but who, in most cases, belong basically to the middle class).

Therefore, nearly 30 million economic entities are not subject to Social Security or income-tax withholding. With their spouses and adult children, they could, if well organized, cast 50 or 60 million votes in any general election—more than sufficient to capture the White House and create a majority in both houses of Congress.

# Why This Middle Class Growth?

I have discussed the nature of the middle class and its phenomenal growth in the U.S.

Why, and how, has this happened? Perhaps I should note, in passing, that one of the basic dogmas of Marxism was that the middle class, under the "laws" of economic determinism and diminishing returns, would be eliminated automatically under inexorable capitalist development. Since this was one of its great fallacies, communists know no way to get rid of the middle class except by force, exile to Siberia and genocidal slaughter.

It is, of course, true that certain industries, such as steel, auto production, mass communication and transportation etc, which require vast concentrations of capital, are beyond middle-class capacity. However, these employ only a small fraction of our entire work force.

Food production (farming), rental housing and retail trade, service establishments, consulting firms and sales organizations, the professions and a great deal of production in the cities, etc., are owned and operated by people who work in businesses where the capital is furnished by the owner-operator.

As I have pointed out, the members of the middle class now total nearly 30 million economic units, compared with a total trade union membership of 21 million, which includes government employees and many others who are actually associated entrepreneurs.

Now why can an independent businessman—for example, a paint and wallpaper dealer—not only survive, but prosper, in the face of competition from the chains and large department stores? He can do so because the employees of the latter have little or no personal interest in the business; they are clock watchers, concerned primarily in their weekly paychecks. Too much attention to the employer's welfare and aggrandizement will only elicit jealousy and hatred from other employees, who are more interested in less work than they are in the profits of the business.

In addition, the overhead, taxes and other costs are horrendous, and they cannot be avoided.

The independent is willing to work 60 or 70 hours a week as the price of success; he knows that hard work and success can lead to independence and even to affluence. Furthermore, the self-employed individual pays far less in Social Security contributions than is demanded for comparable incomes in the form of wages or salaries.

Nor is this by any means all: The IRS, in official testimony before the House Subcommittee on Government Operations on September 5-6, 1979, stated that the self-employed are underreporting taxable income by about 50 percent, which means that many millions of these are keeping tens of billions of dollars that would be exacted from them if they were employees.

Take my experience, for example: I established a paint and wallpaper store in Detroit in 1935 only a block from Sears, Roebuck and Co. and adjacent to a hardware store. I lived on a dollar a day in a room I had constructed in the back of the shop. I worked at least 60 hours a week, and it was three years before I had my first dollar to lay away.

However, at the end of 15 years, I was able to retire with enough so that I could live decently for the remainder of my life on the income from investments.

When I am ready to publish a book, I go to a local typesetter who operates a one-man office in a four-story building in which about 80 other proprietors make their independent livings. Ordinarily, he has enough work to keep him busy. But he takes my jobs on a contract basis and does the work after hours or on weekends. He completes them for less than half of what it would cost in a union shop in New York or Washington. Yes, and he earns more per hour than the union employees make—for the simple reason that he has no additional overhead, nothing is snipped out of his pay, and he has every incentive to produce at a maximum rate.

This is the real story of millions of middle-class proprietors and entrepreneurs. They succeed because they can offer better service and lower prices than can the large corporation with its unionized labor force.

Take the auto mechanic who works 40 hours a week for an employer in a garage: A job he does there may cost the car owner $100; but if the same work is done by the same mechanic in his home workshop for $50, he may well pocket twice as much as he would receive, net, for doing the same work under the direction of his employer.

Since the independent can reduce costs by eliminating much of the tax and overhead burden, nothing less than a socialist or a communist revolution can destroy his capacity to outserve and undersell his corporate competition. I discern, in this, a strong glimmer of hope for the future of the U.S. and the entire Western World.

# Family Business

This is written because a correspondent asked how he might best organize a family business with possibly one employee outside the family circle and with perhaps a net income of $25,000 or $30,000.

Actually, there are three ways in which such an enterprise could be established:

- A corporation;
- A partnership; and
- A simple proprietorship.

**First, a corporation.** Almost any family can create such an entity by following instructions readily available from sources which require little or no aid from an attorney. The state authority, under which corporations are organized, will be happy to supply all necessary information. If this is done, the different members of a family can be issued shares of stock, or all of it can be retained by the man or by spouses.

If dividends are declared, they will be paid to the shareholders. However, since such payments are subject to double taxation, it it usually preferable that any surplus created by the corporation above expenses be disbursed in the form of wages or salaries, which are deductible to the corporation, or in the form of reimbursements, which are tax exempt both to the corporation and to the recipients.

A corporation must make regular income tax returns. However, in most cases, small ones do not retain enough net income to require the payment of income taxes. One advantage of a corporation is that it enjoys limited liability, as do its officers and stockholders. Another is that it can make various deductible expenditures not available to a simple proprietorship.

**PARTNERS**

**Second, a partnership.** This has several attractive features. Although it must make an information return, showing its financial operations, it does not pay any income taxes. There can be any number of partners, who will receive income in proportion to their investment and service. These partners are subject to income taxation, but only as self-employed entities or individuals, whether profits are disbursed or not. Each partner will be subject to a Social Security (SS) tax at the same rate as any other self-employed person.

However, there is no double levy as when an employee-employer relationship exists; and therefore, in 1982, the SS tax for a self-employed individual is only 9.35 percent, as compared to the combined tax of 13.4 percent on an employer and an employee. Thus substantial savings are available for a partnership, in contrast to what applies in the case of a corporation.

If a family of six establishes a partnership which disburses $30,000 in equal amounts, each recipient would owe $467.50 for Social Security in 1982. However, since only $1,700 would be subject to income taxation, even when there is no itemizing, the total of SS and income taxation would be about $4,000—an amount which will be reduced when the 25 percent reduction takes effect in July, 1983. Should a corporation disburse $30,000 in salaries to a married couple with four children, the SS and income taxes would total nearly $9,000.

## PROPRIETOR

**Third, a proprietorship.** A single person or a couple can easily establish a simple proprietorship. No legal documents are necessary, as with a corporation or a partnership. Whoever invests in, and does the work for, such a business, whatever it may be, will be the owner and proprietor.

As in a partnership, the proprietor is a self-employed individual; he or she keeps his own books and prepares all returns. A single person or a couple may act as a single entity. If there are children who perform any service, they should be treated as employees. Under this arrangement, one person or the spouses together act as a self-employed entrepreneur. The pay of the children will not be subject to SS withholding unless they are over 21 years of age. Nor need any be withheld for a spouse.

## IMMUNE

We should note that even if each of the children receives up to $2,300, this will be immune to income tax taxation.

The parents may still take an exemption for each of them on their own return. If the compensation totals $3,300, there will still be no income tax due, but the parents will not be permitted to report them as dependents.

Let us suppose that a couple with four children establishes a proprietorship which disburses $30,000 of profit. Best results will be attainable if each child receives, say, $2,100—a total of $8,400, tax free. The SS tax will be $1,125 for the children and $2,018.80 on the proprietors' income of $21,600. Since their income tax will be—without itemizing—about $2,500 in 1982, the total for all SS and income taxes will be about $5,600.

But remember that since these proprietors will keep their own books and make their own reports, they alone will know what their net and taxable income is—and they will be certain not to overpay.

In summary, if individuals or couples operate a small business, a simple proprietorship is the best form. If children are to be integrated into the business, a partnership might be most desirable. If there are large investments, especially in real estate, I believe it would be best to organize a corporation.

Many years ago, when I established my paint store, it was a simple proprietorship. A number of years later, when the assets had grown to many times the original, I organized a corporation. I think that each form was best at the time I established it. About 15 years later, I dissolved the corporation, with considerable benefit to myself.

Everyone should carefully evaluate and consider his own situation and needs, and establish his business in the form that will, for him, be most productive and economical.

# Review of Populists

Readers of The SPOTLIGHT will recall that in 1980, a series of articles appeared that discussed in detail the contributions and beliefs of various great populists in American history. These included Thomas Jefferson, Andrew Jackson, Bob LaFollette Sr., Thomas E. Watson, Henry Ford, Hiram Johnson, "Alfalfa Bill" Murray, Robert R. McCormick, Burton K. Wheeler, Hamilton Fish, George W. Malone, Charles E. Coughlin and Charles A. Lindbergh. These articles have now been published in a volume called "Profiles in Populism,"* which I recommend to all readers.

The true populist philosophy—as expressed by these men—holds a generally unified point of view. Thomas Jefferson, in my opinion, stands first and foremost. His ideals constituted the basis on which this nation was founded; his was a revolutionary economic and social concept, which made America the greatest, freest and most prosperous and powerful nation on earth.

Some have confused populism with socialism or other totalitarian movements. This is a complete error, for true populism stands foursquare for individualism, freedom from control, and personal reliance and responsibility. It always projects individual rights in opposition to collective control and tyranny.

**MIDDLE CLASS**

This leads directly to the crucial concept of middle-class importance in society. This group may be defined as consisting of all those, regardless of source of income, who earn their own living, support themselves and their families, pay their share of taxes and make no trouble for the law enforcement agencies.

In a somewhat narrower concept, it consists of the self-employed—farmers, professionals, proprietors, consultants, salesmen, operators of income property and several other categories. Since independent farmers constituted the great majority of American citizens in Colonial times, it was possible to create the form of government established here.

One fact emerges above all others in this political spectrum: Those who earn their living by operating their own investment property must make correct economic decisions in order to prosper or even to survive; and only those who do this are likely to think for themselves in the political sphere. Therefore, they constitute the bedrock upon which every republican and responsible form of government must rest.

Thus, a basic conflict emerges: Those who drive for central control hate and fear the middle class and seek to destroy or impoverish it. This includes socialists, communists, labor bosses, bureaucrats, monopoly capitalists, the great financiers and every central government as it usurps more and more power and control.

**DESIDERATA**

What, then, does the middle class desire? First, a strictly limited and thrifty central government, which will not take from the producers the wealth they create to support parasites, either rich or poor. They want no largesse themselves from the state, but they want freedom from its regulations.

They believe fervently in free enterprise, a system in which every individual will be encouraged to develop his highest capacities and in which he will be fully compensated for his efforts and success. Like Jefferson, they believe in an aristocracy of virtue and talent, which develops naturally from among the people when all are given the opportunity to rise and to be rewarded for success.

Although the middle class knows that some will be rich and others poor, it seeks to prevent the aggrandizement of the former through legalized robbery. It opposes a central welfare state in which the exploiting elite tax the middle class so that it can purchase the votes of idle parasites and thus perpetuate itself in power and position.

Specifically, populists agree that:

● Our Federal Reserve System and Internal Revenue Service (IRS) are perversions of our Constitution and should be replaced; and

● Our monetary policies and taxation should be for the benefit of the people, instead of a powerful and shadowy "plunderbund."

It believes that those who exert themselves in private enterprise should enjoy the fruits of their labor. It believes in real freedom of speech, of the press and of assembly in all respects, especially in significant areas, in which an almost total blackout now exists because of centralized control over the media and our educational institutions.

It believes that we should have more independent proprietors; that they should be encouraged to succeed; and that they should never be hampered, harassed, and destroyed by the government, especially the IRS. It considers the fact that more than 60 percent of the wealth now created by the producers goes for interest and taxes constitutes a total subversion of the ideals left us by our Founding Fathers.

**TRANQUILITY**

"Populism," we read in the introduction to our book, "is a force for stability, creating a tranquil society in which individual and cultural growth can occur without the progress being threatened by alien forces promoting culture distortion."

The American middle class is therefore nationalistic. Like Jefferson, it has not one farthing of interest outside its own country. It believes in self-defense, but rejects foreign military adventurism, which kills or maims our youth and creates enormous and inextinguishable debts.

The middle class rejects the internationalism which seeks to destroy our heritage by dividing our people into two classes, the super rich on the one hand and the propertyless proletarians on the other; which promotes deflation and inflation in order to accomplish its sinister objectives. The middle class embraces a nationalism which will place America always first and refuse to meld us into a "new world order" under the control of the international financiers.

The middle class is conscious of its social heritage. While it holds that every ethnic group has a right to its own integrity, diversity in a population is a part of populist philosophy.

It opposes all forms of slavery; condemns the exploitation of one class or group by another; but believes that each has a right to pursue its own objectives in any way that does not harm others.

It knows, furthermore, that the myth of equality is a fairy tale. It therefore opposes special privileges for minorities and seeks to prevent a vast influx of aliens from Africa, the Caribbean, Mexico, South Asia and other areas where the people have been able to do little or nothing to accomplish their own development.

This, in part, constitutes the philosophy of the middle class. Study "Profiles in Populism" for a more detailed account of what it involves. ▼

---

*"Profiles in Populism" is available for $12.95 hardback and $7.95 in soft-cover from Liberty Library, 300 Independence Ave., S.E., Washington, D.C. 20003.

# Harassment of Private Business

Early in 1942 while I was operating a paint store in Detroit and shortly after I had purchased an apartment building, I first became fully aware of the fact that the federal bureaucracy is constantly at war against small independent enterprise. The OPA (Office of Price Administration) established by the Roosevelt administration had as its principal objective the destruction and extirpation of independent business and private investment from the American scene.

It was simply following the socialist-communist doctrines and policies advocated by John Maynard Keynes, the English theoretician, who declared that all private investment income should be eliminated by a gradual process of economic euthanasia. When the "wartime emergency" controls were finally ended **eight** years after WW II, some 8 million small property owners had lost their investments, which they had hoped would furnish some income during their retirement years.

The federal bureaucracy is the sworn enemy of private business, especially the smaller independent variety. It does everything within its power to regulate, harass, strangle, and destroy. A businessman must file endless reports, submit to supervision and examination, pay exorbitant taxes, and engage in frequent and costly battles with the Internal Revenue Service, which may result in his economic destruction or even in early death.

Why? Because:
* (1) The independent cannot be adequately policed;
* (2) His income cannot be accurately determined; and
* (3) Most of all, he desires no favors from government; tends to think for himself politically, and therefore cannot be either bribed or controlled.

One of the more recent attempts to strangle private business took form in what was known as OSHA (Occupational Safety and Health Administration), which empowered federal inspectors to enter the premises of any private business, enforce the most ridiculous rules and regulations, levy huge fines, and, as a result, literally force hundreds of thousands of entrepreneurs out of business. However, a number of brave and hardy patriots began resisting this monster, and one after another were successful in forcing inspectors to obtain search warrants, stating probable cause why any particular location should be searched and inspected.

Before me lies a letter from a Liberty Lobby supporter who operates a business in Georgia. He had refused entry to an OSHA inspector, who thereupon sought an order in the U.S. District Court in Atlanta to enforce an examination of the premises. Since no probable cause could be established, the court denied OSHA the power it demanded; and when the decision was appealed to the Fifth U.S. Circuit Court of Appeals in New Orleans, F.R. Marshall, the U.S. Secretary of Labor, asked that the OSHA appeal be dismissed.

This was a very important victory for independent business. I suspect that the government itself asked for dismissal so that the case would not go to the Supreme Court, where a final judgment would probably have outlawed OSHA entirely.

Let me point out that the desire to conduct independent business constitutes an irrepressible urge among our strongest and most patriotic citizens. In spite of every attempt on the part of the federal bureaucracy to repress and destroy it, the number of entrepreneurs increased from 5.6 million in 1945 to more than 13 million in 1980, and their income and economic significance to an even greater degree. For this and other similar reasons I believe that the future of this nation is not hopeless.

# Ch. 3
# Audits, Restrictions, and Defenses

# IRS Bureaucracy

The annual appropriations by Congress for the operation of the Internal Revenue Service are now approaching $9 billion a year—nine times as much as it cost to run the entire federal government in the 1920s.

The Service has about 82,000 employees, of whom some 17,000 are auditing agents. All of these must bring in at least $200 for every hour spent in audits—otherwise the whole procedure becomes counter-productive. After all, these men must bring in enough to pay not only for their own keep and overhead, but also for those of the other 65,000 IRS employees.

A little arithmetic will demonstrate how this works: if all of these work 250 days, eight hours a day, they will put in 32 million man-hours a year; at $300 an hour, they will collect $9.6 billion—only slightly more than they cost the taxpayers.

Every time a taxpayer forces the IRS to put in two hours or 10 hours instead of one to collect $100, he has done something toward sending the IRS to its ultimate oblivion. If a million taxpayers will compel it to expend 20 million man-hours without result, its doom will soon be sealed.

When IRS officials go before a congressional committee to obtain increased appropriations so that more agents can be hired to extort money from additional taxpayers, nothing is said about the illegal and unethical—even criminal—methods used to obtain an average of about $800 from millions of taxpayers.

All they emphasize is that for every dollar of additional appropriations, they are able to produce $2 to $5 of extra revenue for the Treasury. Actually, much of this is obtained by methods that make Al Capone seem like a saint and are more comparable to those used by the Roman government during the time of Herod in Judea who commissioned highway men to rob travellers and caravans on condition that they return one-half of the loot to the authorities.

However, and fortunately, there are powerful and influential people who do not like to be robbed and who have therefore forced the government to place certain protective provisions into the Internal Revenue Code.

The agency hopes that the average citizen, especially the small businessman, will not be aware of these or will find them too expensive, and will therefore not be able to use them. But they are there to protect him as well as the rich and the super-rich. It requires some time and study, but it is certain that the IRS can be defeated wholly or at least in part; it has been done myriads of times.

Any literate taxpayer who will concentrate on his dispute, may well discover, not only that he can be victorious, but that he can obtain a valuable education in tax-law and procedures, which will confer upon him a sense of elation he could not otherwise hope to enjoy.

# IRS Auditing Trickery

As indicated last week, the IRS collects various sums not due from millions of taxpayers every year by the use of trickery—usually by persuading its victims that the Code contains provisions which are not there. However, more and more people are now learning how to defend themselves successfully, and doing it themselves.

Let us consider the case of John Q. Taxslave, who has made full disclosure and, to the best of his belief and knowledge, paid all taxes due. Now the IRS calls and says it is to make a "routine" audit.

He should not be deceived by this honeyed talk: there is no such thing. The IRS does not make an audit unless it hopes to collect more money, especially by the use of some snare or trap in the code. Here is what the taxpayer should do:

• Tell the agent that he will not communicate with him or make any agreement over the telephone, but that everything must be in writing.

• When he receives a letter suggesting a date for the audit, he should answer this by saying (a) that it must take place at his own convenience and at his own home or office; (b) that he must be told in advance precisely what facts are to be verified; and (c) that nothing else is to be discussed.

• If the taxpayer finds the date suggested for the audit inconvenient. he should write a letter so stating and suggesting another time. He can do this two or three times. He should send all communications by certified mail, return receipt requested.

• The taxpayer should never permit any of his records to leave his own custody nor should he permit an IRS agent to make any copies of them.

• Since the courts have held that a taxpayer's records in the custody of another are subject to examination or seizure, such documents should never be left with a CPA, a bookkeeper, or attorney.

• During the audit, the agent should be permitted to examine cancelled checks and invoices which are necessary to verify expenditures and allowances, and only once.

• If the agent attempts a "fishing expedition" into other materials, he should be told politely but firmly that this will not be permitted.

• During the audit, the taxpayer should never volunteer any information of any kind. He should say nothing except what is absolutely necessary to support the verification of his deductions.

# Privacy Act of 1974

The Freedom of Information Act of 1966 and the Privacy Act of 1974 are, when properly used, powerful tools in the hands of both taxpayers and tax-resisters.

The former provides that, upon request, each government agency must supply every citizen with any and all documents it has in its possession dealing directly or indirectly with his relation to the Internal Revenue Service. It places the burden of proof upon the government and can easily be employed by the citizen.

For example, if a citizen is arrested for failure to file a proper income tax return and brought to trial on this charge, he is entitled to learn why he is being prosecuted while others are ignored.

He can also compel the government to turn over all manuals, special directives, etc., which bear in any way on the pending prosecution. Most of all, he can force the government to surrender every item of information it has gathered about him through surveillance, phone-tapping, mail coverage, interviews with third parties, or any other source whatever.

The Privacy Act is even more important: the IRS is now required to print a summary of this in its "Instructions on Form 1040," and it reads as follows:

"The Privacy Act of 1974 provides that each federal agency inform individuals, whom it asks to supply information, of the authority for the solicitation of the information and whether disclosure of such information is mandatory or voluntary; the principal purpose or purposes for which the information is to be used; the routine uses which may be made of the information; and the effects on the individual of not providing the requested information. This notification applies to the U.S. individual income tax returns, to declarations of estimated tax, to U.S. gift tax returns, and to any other tax return required to be filed by an individual . . ."

If the taxpayer utilizes this properly, it will prevent any "fishing expedition" on the part of the IRS—a tactic which it loves so dearly and which it has employed so extensively and often with such destructive results. We remember when it could compel the taxpayer preceding an audit to complete the notorious Ten-Year Net-Worth Statement on pain of immediate confiscation.

Now, it cannot even ask a simple question without citing chapter and verse as authority for so doing; it must explain what it intends to do with any information it desires or obtains; whether it is voluntary or compulsory; and what will happen to the taxpayer if he declines to answer.

Properly used, the Freedom of Information and Privacy Acts will put a summary end to a large portion of all IRS activities which have been routine ever since the agency became a curse to the American people under Franklin Delano Roosevelt.

# Freedom of Information Act

In 1966, Congress passed the Freedom of Information Act; and in 1974, after hearings at which I testified, the Act was amended. I proposed that every government agency having data in its files concerning any citizen be required to notify such individual of the fact and release the material in full on request.

However, Congress compromised and wrote into law only that every government agency must release any material it may have concerning anyone when the individual involved demands that this be done.

The other day a man wrote wanting to know what to do when the IRS fails or refuses to release information after it receives a written request to do so. We have received detailed reports from various individuals who have demanded the release of such materials.

They state that the IRS—while not refusing outright to comply with the law—usually shunts the citizen around from one office or jurisdiction to another and, with excuse after excuse, continues to delay compliance.

It seems that non-compliance by the IRS is a very different matter from non-compliance by the taxpayer, who cannot bring the same awesome force and power of a government with inexhaustible finances and manpower to bear upon an opponent.

But to continue: after patient persistence, the citizen is finally able to pry loose from the Service a certain portion of the documents relating to himself; but invariably, he is told that there are exceptions and exemptions which permit the withholding of certain information for reasons which, to say the least, are extremely vague. The citizen is of course convinced that the unreleased material is precisely that which is most crucial and which would, without doubt, reveal that the IRS had engaged in criminal activities.

A syndicated article in the Arizona "Republic" states that in 1976 about 150,000 demands were made upon government agencies to release information in their files.

Of these, "25,000 were denied in whole or in part. About 4,200 of these denials produced appeals, and about 3,700 were decided in that year. In about 12 per cent of the cases, part of the information was released."

Again, we find that the federal government is by far the greatest lawbreaker in the country. The Freedom of Information Act holds that all personal information, unless the national security might be endangered, must be released upon request within 40 days. Routinely, delays occur running into several months; and even then only a part—and never the really sensitive portion—of the information sought is released.

In order to make the Freedom of Information Act truly effective, every government agency should be required to notify every citizen of any material it may have concerning him in its files; and heavy fines and/or prison terms should be imposed upon any bureaucrat personally who fails or refuses to obey the law.

The agencies now complain that compliance with FOIA provisions takes an enormous amount of time: well, they didn't complain that it took too much time when they were gathering the information—in fact that they were even doing so was a prime secret.

In the meantime, every person who does not receive complete and prompt satisfaction should sue the agency involved; and then we should bring pressure upon Congress to put more teeth in the law.

# Section 7609—IRS Code

One correspondent asked what law the IRS could cite during the year 1976 by which to obtain bank and other records pertinent to a taxpayer. The answer is that, despite several adverse court decisions, particularly **Reisman v. Caplin**, 375 U.S., decided June 15, 1964, the service proceeded under Section 7210 of the Code, which was supported by several other provisions therein, and which conferred upon it the power to obtain **any** records whatsoever from anyone; the threatened punishment for failure or refusal to produce was a fine of $1,000 and a prison term of one year.

However, this is now completely changed. As explained in detail in my manual,* Section 7609 was added to the Code in the Tax Reform Act of 1976, effective January 1, 1977, which has established the following procedures:

(1) If the IRS seeks any records relevant to a taxpayer held by any third party, that agency must send a notice of such action to the taxpayer within three days after making the request to the third party.

(2) The taxpayer then has 20 days in which to write the IRS and the record-holder that he objects to such examination.

(3) **The IRS may then ask a United States District Court to order such an examination.**

(4) If such a request is made, a hearing will result in which the IRS must show probable cause and at which the taxpayer may appear to interpose his objections.

(5) Should the District Court rule in favor of the IRS, the taxpayer can appeal the decision to the Circuit Court of Appeals--and even to the Supreme Court.

All this is a long-drawn-out and cumbersome procedure and one in which the IRS will engage only if large stakes are involved. Meanwhile, it cannot take one peek at any records held by a bank, a lawyer, a CPA, an accountant, or anyone else. This situation is indeed a far cry from that in which an IRS agent walked into a bank or an accountant's office, drew up a brief vest-pocket summons (Form 2039-A) and forthwith proceeded to examine, rummage through, and make copies of any document which he desired to duplicate . . . all without the knowledge of the taxpayer.

In addition to all this, we should note that the "third party" can force the IRS to pay the cost of preparing the documents. I know of one case in which it took the IRS three years to obtain the necessary court sanction, and then, when faced with a $300 charge for preparation, decided to get along without the documents after all.

Any recordholder or taxpayer who now permits the IRS to examine documents without first getting the approval of the Circuit Court of Appeals has simply fallen prey and victim to the bluff or the illegal procedures of the Internal Revenue Service.

---

*"How to Defend Yourself Against the IRS," available for $175.00 from Government Educational Foundation, Box 1622, Washington, D.C. 20013; price includes automatic three-year subscription to all supplements and changes.

# Preventing an IRS Rip-Off

If taxpayers would observe and enforce the following rules during and following their audits, the great IRS ripoff of obedient taxpayers would come to an end.

• During the audit, have a witness present, which is officially permitted in "IRS Publication 556," although the agent will often attempt to deny this privilege. And, even though the Service hates tape-recorders like a plague, it cannot prevent their use. Be sure you have one in operation which will record every word spoken by the agent during the conference.

• Demand that he sign with his own name any paper or document he leaves with you; be sure to write down his name and service number; but never sign anything he places before you except on the advice of reliable counsel or after you are absolutely certain that it will not be used to harm you.

• If he states you have violated any provision of the IRS Code or regulations, demand that he show you the document which he claims as his authority. If he says that you owe money for any reason, demand that he produce the section or subsection of the Code which supports the allegation. If he declares that some provision in his manual is his authority, require him to show you this and give you a copy of it.

• If he says that you have violated any law, demand that he show and give you all documents in his possession which support his position.

• If he continues to harass you, prepare a document summarizing your experiences and send this to your congressman, your two senators, and to the current chairman of the Senate Appropriations Committee, In some instances, it might be expedient to send it also to your daily newspaper for publication in the Letters to the Editor column.

• As long as you are on firm ground and feel that the IRS is demanding money not due or more than is due, do not fear publicity, for this is something that IRS dreads more than almost anything else. Nor does it like to explain to senators or congressmen why it is harassing a taxpayer.

• Your best defense depends on your determination to fight for your rights and to do so, not only with IRS personnel, but also in the political arena and in the public press.

# 'The Master Tax Guide'

Sales, excise, import, export, and property taxes totalling more than $100 billion were collected in 1974; and all the laws, regulations and court decisions dealing with them could probably be printed in a few pages.

However, when we arrive in the jungle known as the federal income tax, we find that there are 80,000 bureaucrats who cost the taxpayers about $9 billion; that the taxpayers themselves spend perhaps $8 billion just to prepare their returns and to defend themselves against the IRS, in addition to all taxes which they pay.

The Commerce Clearing House offers an edition of the Internal Revenue Code in paperback for $19.00; and a companion volume called "The Master Tax Guide" for $13.78. Any taxpayer who tangles with the IRS should have at least these volumes at his disposal.*

**The Code itself comprises nearly 2,000 pages of fine print with sections numbered from 1 to 9,042. Most of these have subsections, paragraphs, and subparagraphs in endless profusion.**

There are references and cross-references in bewildering complexity. The language of most of the provisions is such that a superior Ph.D. can read them many times without grasping their meaning.

The IRS agents do not pretend to understand it; members of Congress are as innocent of knowledge concerning it as a new-born babe; justices of the Supreme Court cannot agree as to its meaning.

And yet, unless the businessman who must spend 12 hours a day and 70 hours a week to sustain his enterprise is versed in all its traps and snares, he may perhaps some day be reduced to pauperism because of them.

**However, even the "Master Tax Guide" is only the vestibule to this esoteric domain. There are 40,000 pages of regulations, most of them unpublished, which are nevertheless cited as if they were law duly passed by Congress. In addition, there is "West's Annotated U.S. Code, Title 26," where the researcher may find tens of thousands of court decisions dealing with the multitudinous sections of the Code.**

If a man were to do nothing for ten years except devote himself to an intensive study of this jungle, he would still be only a beginner in its mysteries.

Every year, the demand for simplification of income-tax returns rises from a weary and frustrated nation. Every year, this is promised. And then, every year, as regularly as the motion of the earth, the returns become more intricate, more extensive, more difficult to understand or complete.

---

***These volumes are available in most major bookstores. However, if you cannot find them locally, contact Commerce Clearing House, 4025 W. Peterson Ave., Chicago, Ill. 60646.**

# *Beating the IRS  Auditing Game*

Terrible as are the gins and snares planted in the Code for the purpose of destroying individuals who may succeed in free enterprise, they are not the only bombs used for the same purpose by the IRS. If it does not have a ready-made trap in the Code applicable to given case, it may invent one, and proceed with gusto in its joyful task of ruining the honest businessman who has paid all his taxes.

An agent, let us say, has completed his "routine" audit, and found nothing on which to hang an additional assessment; in short, his labors have been wholly in vain. Faced with such a tragic frustration, he searches his mendacious brain for some means of extracting money from his innocent prey.

For example, if the man reported his income properly on either an accrual or cash basis, the agent may tell his victim that he must switch to the other, if thereby he can levy an additional tax. Or he will go through his itemized deductions and arbitrarily disallow a number of these, no matter how valid they may be.

There are countless methods such as these by which to extract additional money. I have known an agent to tell a taxpayer that a commission paid to a real estate company was not deductible because it is a loss realized but not recognized! I have known an agent to maintain that royalties are subject to the self-employment tax.

I would say this: let us beat these clever boys at their own game. Fortunately, there are administrative procedures open to everyone, poor, middle-income, and rich. When an assessment is questionable, even if it involves only one dollar, it is the patriotic duty of the taxpayer to demand a conference at the district level; if he does not obtain satisfaction there, he can and should go to the Appellate level, where, with some preparation, he may be offered a very good compromise.

If he does not win what he thinks is his right there, he can go to the Tax Court without benefit of expensive counsel. He should obtain a copy of a book called Rules of Practice and Procedure in the United States Tax Court, which can be obtained from the Government Printing Office, for $1.10. This will tell any intelligent person what to do and how to do it. This step, of course, involves considerable effort and preparation; but if millions would avail themselves of this procedure—as they can—we would tie up the administrative machinery of the IRS so completely that it would cease to function.

**And this is what we should do!**

# Business and Investment Privacy

We know one couple who has achieved complete privacy by having only self-employment income, living in furnished apartments which have no tenant-rosters, moving two or three times a year, maintaining no bank accounts in their own names, and having their mail sent to a box in care of a corporation. They have paid no income tax or made any returns for years; and they feel assured of lifetime immunity and privacy.

Let us summarize some of the techniques used to insure privacy by an increasing number of people. Many carry no substantial bank balances; and, if they have checking accounts, they keep these at very low levels and draw upon them only for payments which would be of no interest to the IRS anyway such as utility bills.

When they receive checks, they cash them at the issuing banks or use them to pay obligations by endorsing them over to third parties.

Some people simply buy travellers' checks in quantities and make all payments by means of them, rather than by personal check. As Mark Skousen notes in an article dealing with this subject, Swiss Bankers Travellers checks are particularly desirable, not only because of the anonymity they confer, but also in that they are constantly increasing in value as the American dollar continues its rapid decline.

Another method to prevent IRS intrusion is using non-reproducible checks made of dark red paper. These can be obtained from Liberty Graphics, P.O. Box 3614, Charlotte, N.C. 28203. Others advocate the use of a certain kind of ink in writing checks which will not photograph under microfilming.

Still another method to achieve privacy is the use of a foreign checking account, for example in Canada, Mexico, or certain European countries. However, care should be used in establishing such accounts, as the U.S. law requires that their existence be divulged.

Mexico is a good country in which to leave deposits, since no bank there will provide any information concerning them to anyone whatever.

One favorite means of securing privacy is the purchase of gold bullion or coins (preferably Krugerrands), and keeping them secreted in a safe place. Or, such assets can be stored with responsible institutions in London or elsewhere at a very small fee; they will purchase and/or sell such coins or bullion at the behest of the investor and there will be no report of such transactions to any government authority.

Other types of investments not only assure privacy, but also avoid taxation with complete legality. Among these, tax-exempt bonds are perhaps the most important, of which there are now some $500 billion in existence in the U.S., enough for $5,000 for every household in the country and nearly $8,000 for every taxpaying unit. There is no official record of transactions involving their transfer; there are no known rosters of owners; no reports are made to the IRS of payments.

The holders of such unregistered bonds—which are somewhat similar to what $5,000 interest-bearing Federal Reserve notes would be like—simply clip the coupons, cash or deposit them at any bank or savings and loan association, and do whatever they wish with the proceeds. Should any IRS agent ask whether you have such securities, it is your privilege to inform him that this is none of his business, since income from them is excludable from gross (i.e., reportable) income, under Sec. 115 of the Internal Revenue Code.

# The Protective Audit

Let us consider the case of the taxpayer who has filed a conventional return, faces the prospect of an audit, and merely wishes to protect himself against IRS bluff and abuse.

When he receives a telephone call proposing an audit, he will state that all communications must be in writing. When a letter arrives demanding that the taxpayer appear at the IRS office with all his records, he will reply that the time suggested is not convenient and that the conference must take place at his own home or office at a time suitable for him. He can postpone the conference at least two or three times.

Before he agrees to meet with the agent, the taxpayer will insist that he receive an exact list of the items or deductions to be discussed or verified. When the agent appears at the appointed place, he will face also two or more of the taxpayer's friends, who will not only act as witnesses but may also be empowered to speak for him (Publication 556). Or he may have his accountant, lawyer, or tax-preparer present.

He will also have at least two tape recorders in operation so that, if the IRS agent demands it, one cassette may be made for him. Federal judges have declared that the taxpayer may use such devices, provided a tape is also made available to the IRS. If the agent refuses to begin or continue the conference if it is recorded, the taxpayer is within his rights to refuse to confer without such recording.

The taxpayer will offer no unnecessary information nor engage in any irrelevant conversation. He will not permit any "fishing expedition." He will read the provisions of the Privacy Act (printed in all IRS 1040 instruction manuals) to the agent and thus force him to cite his authority for any question he asks.

He will not permit the agent to copy any document, remove it from the premises, or investigate the return for any year more than once. If an audit results in no additional tax, the taxpayer may not be audited during the ensuing year except under unusual conditions. The taxpayer will never sign any paper the agent places before him, unless he is absolutely certain that no harm will result.

If the taxpayer is not satisfied with any determination the agent makes, he can demand and obtain a conference in the district office. If he believes that any tax demanded there is excessive or illegal, he can go to the Appellate Division. If he is still not satisfied, he can go to the Tax "Court" with little or no aid from an accountant or attorney.

He can even go to the Circuit Court of Appeals without paying any tax demanded by the IRS. The records indicate that most deficiencies are settled at about 40 cents on the dollar in the Appellate Division and at 30 cents in the Tax "Court." In a great many cases, the taxpayer not only defeats the IRS completely but gets rid of its harassment permanently.

The taxpayer should never pay a questionable levy just because it is easier than to do battle or cheaper than to hire a competent defender. If a taxpayer remits without protest, he will be marked for annual extortion. On the other hand, if he fights the agency successfully, it will probably leave him alone in the future.

# Confronting an IRS Agent

Many taxpayers have asked me what methods they should use to defend themselves.

When I have been asked that question by taxpayers, I tell them that if they would like to obtain a practical education and gain self-confidence by fighting their own battles, they should first obtain an up-to-date copy of the Internal Revenue Code and study all the provisions dealing with any dispute in which they may be involved with the service.

They should also obtain a copy of "The Master Tax Guide," published by the Commerce Clearing House, which is very useful because it translates into more simplified language what is stated in the obscurantist mysticism of the code, which is intended to be utterly unintelligible even to the bureaucrats who administer it.

I tell taxpayers further that, if they are willing to permit an agent to examine their records at all, the following procedures should be followed:

● If an agent calls on the phone stating that he wishes to conduct an audit, he should be told that no communications may be carried on except in writing.

● When a letter arrives from the agent, the taxpayer should reply (by certified mail, return receipt requested) that any conference must take place at a place and time convenient for the taxpayer.

● Previous to such conference, agent must submit in writing an exact list of what he wishes to know or what facts he wishes verified or why.

● No other investigation will be permitted.

● The taxpayer should never agree to bring his records to the IRS office; when the agent arrives at the home or office of the taxpayer, it must be at an appointed time—should he come at any other, he will not be admitted and there will be no conversation.

The taxpayer has a right, according to IRS Publication 556, to have witnesses present at any conference. The taxpayer must in no circumstances permit the agent to copy any document or to remove it from the taxpayer's premises. Furthermore, the agent is prohibited under his own law to re-audit the return of any given year.

If he then refuses to continue the conference, the taxpayer is within his rights if he declares that the agency has exhausted its authority to examine the return for the year involved.

At this point, the agent may decide to disallow some of the taxpayer's deductions, or to base additional assessments on other redeterminations. When this is done, the district office must explain precisely what changes are proposed and why.

The taxpayer will now consult, not only the code and "The Master Tax Guide," but he will also go to a library containing West's "United States Code, Annotated, Title 26," or a similar compendium and discover what the courts have said in regard to the section or subsection under dispute. He may be surprised at how completely in error the IRS agent has been.

The taxpayer will then contest every new assessment: first in a district office conference; second, with a conferee at the local level; third, in the Appellate Court; and, fourth, in the Tax Court itself. The Tax Court pretends to be apart from and independent of the Internal Revenue Service, but it is a creation of the IRS Code. However, this is a court of record, although no jury trials are available even there.

Publication 556 explains how all these appeals may be made up to and through the Tax Court.

By following this course of action, you can do what innumerable others have done: defend yourself successfully and emerge triumphant over the IRS—a victory comparable to what our Founding Fathers achieved over the tyranny of the English government.

# Defending an IRS Audit

Now that income-tax time is drawing near, a great many people are probably wondering what their chances are of being audited and how they can defend themselves should the IRS question their reported deductions.

Consider that the IRS has about 18,000 auditing agents; that, of 83,343,000 returns filed in 1974, 16,095,000 had no taxable income; 29,726,000 itemized deductions; and 37,522,000 paid a tax but used only the standard deduction.

Now if 18,000 agents were to audit every return with itemized deductions, each would have to conduct 1,651 audits annually, or about 6 each working day. The fact is, that only about 1 or 1.5 million are subjected to audits, on about 70 percent of which additional assessments are made—most of which would never be paid if the taxpayers knew how to defend themselves and did so resourcefully.

There is nothing more likely to trigger an audit than what the IRS considers excessive deductions; we therefore suggest than when large deductions are reported, the taxpayer be prepared to verify these—should the final necessity arise—with invoices and cancelled checks.

There is little likelihood that a return will be selected for audit unless the deductions are substantially in excess of the norm. The **Master Tax Guide**, published by Commerce Clearing House, which works in close collaboration with the Internal Revenue Service, prints a chart in its 1977 edition, Section 1070, which reveals the following statistics:

## AVERAGE ITEMIZED DEDUCTIONS FROM ADJUSTED GROSS INCOME

| Income Classes | Contributions | Interest | Taxes | Medical Expense | Total: Percent of A.G.I. |
|---|---|---|---|---|---|
| $5,000-$6,000 | $312 | $786 | $ 631 | $ 751 | 43% |
| 6,000-7,000 | 434 | 838 | 696 | 695 | 37 |
| 7,000-8,000 | 307 | 911 | 767 | 698 | 35 |
| 8,000-9,000 | 317 | 879 | 780 | 615 | 31 |
| 9,000-10,000 | 326 | 950 | 791 | 533 | 28 |
| 10,000-15,000 | 364 | 1,153 | 1,013 | 506 | 25 |
| 15,000-20,000 | 416 | 1,360 | 1,361 | 404 | 21 |
| 20,000-25,000 | 517 | 1,516 | 1,722 | 409 | 19 |
| 25,000-30,000 | 643 | 1,786 | 2,123 | 402 | 19 |
| 30,000-50,000 | 921 | 2,262 | 2,897 | 497 | 18 |
| 50,000-100,000 | 2,005 | 3,871 | 4,952 | 651 | 18 |
| 100,000 or more | 9,630 | 12,074 | 12,361 | 989 | 20 |

Percentages have probably remained about the same since 1974; but we can be sure that the average dollar amounts now deducted have increased substantially with inflation.

We repeat that unless there is some other reason for conducting an audit, the IRS will probably not disturb any taxpayer unless he exceeds quite substantially the ratios indicated above as the norm from his tax-bracket.

# *Preparing Returns*

I suggested to a tax preparer that since he is one who prepares tax-returns for others for specific fees, he might solve his problem by not establishing definite charges for his work and not actually preparing the documents himself. I said that instead of asking a definite fee, he might suggest that a free-will gift would be appreciated when received from friends, who would merely receive help and direction in making out their own returns.

Thus, he would not be working primarily in the preparation of returns. Nor would he inscribe his name or Social Security number therein. All writing would be done by the taxpayer or a typist; the IRS would never know that anyone except the taxpayer was involved.

Two years later, this man reported that the system worked very well; that very few of his friends had been audited; that none of them had paid any additional taxes; and that their free-will gifts to him were approximately equal to his previous fees and emoluments.

Last summer, I received a letter from Yates H. Barnette of Greenville, Tennessee, who declared that he had been "preparing returns" for 44 years but had never placed his name thereon. "When I did a return," he wrote, "I always told the person or business that I was not making charge for my work, but **IF** they wished to leave a contribution, it would be appreciated. And that is what happened each year."

Finally, however, the IRS tried to crack down on Barnette. The agency threatened to audit his own returns and attempted to compel him to reveal the names and addresses of all his "clients." After discovering some of these, they audited them; but no one would sign a statement that Barnette had charged for his services.

Eventually, the IRS hauled Barnette into the United States District Court for the Eastern District of Tennessee. However, since the government could not produce a single witness who would swear that he had been charged a fee, Judge Guy W. Blackwell approved a motion to dismiss the IRS action on March 28, 1979; and the IRS sent an official letter to the tax-preparer that his own returns had been accepted as rendered.

We should all be grateful to Barnette for his courage and victory. I suggest that independent "tax-preparers" emulate his technique:

● Do not charge any specific fee for services;

● Suggest, instead, that a free-will gift would be appreciated;

● Have taxpayer write in his own figures on the forms, or have them typed in so that the "preparer's" handwriting may appear nowhere on the form;

● Do not place your own name or Social Security number on the return;

● Have your "friends" leave statements that they were not required to pay a fee, nor did they do so; and

● Keep a list of your "friends," including their last names only.

Since any money received in this manner constitutes a gift, it is doubtful that it need be reported as income; this would be true especially if some of the "friends" received the same service without leaving any contribution at all. This would establish the fact that the service was independent of any compensation.

# Restrictions on Tax Preparers

In the Tax Reform Act of 1976, provisions were added to the code to place all private tax-preparers in a strait jacket. (It is interesting to note that IRS agents who prepare tax returns will not even place their names on the form.)

Section 7701 (c) (36) defines private tax-preparers. Sec. 6060 (a) provides that if any person hires others to work as tax-preparers, he must disclose the name, Social Security number, and office address of each such employee in annual reports; 6107 provides that preparers must give taxpayers copies of returns prepared by them and retain copies for their files or at least a list of all clients; 7407 gives the IRS authority to enjoin any tax-preparer from continuing in his work.

Sec. 7216 (c) provides that if any person—private preparer or IRS official—uses any information contained in any return except to prepare the same, he shall be guilty of a misdemeanor and subject to a fine of $1,000 or a year in prison or both, in addition to paying for the cost of prosecution; 6694-95 provide that if any income-tax preparer fails to comply with section 6107 (a), he shall be fined $25.00 for each such failure. If the preparer fails to sign the return or include his Social Security number on it, he shall be fined $25.00 for each such omission. If any preparer fails to retain copies of all returns he prepares or a list of all clients served, he shall be subject to a fine of $50.00 for each such failure, with a maximum penalty of $25,000 for any single return period. If any employer of income-tax preparers fails (or neglects) to comply with the requirement of section 6060, he shall be fined $100 for each such failure, with a maximum fine of $20,000. If any income-tax preparer endorses or otherwise negotiates any check made in respect to taxes or refunds for taxes, he shall be subject to a fine of $500 for each such act.

In addition to these strictures, several states impose others of their own. Altogether these laws and regulations have income-tax preparers under total bureaucratic control—something which those who first proposed the 16th Amendment certainly never visualized.

I have spoken to a number of tax-consultants who would rather go out of business or make a living digging ditches than conform to all these requirements. More than a year ago, I told one of these: "Well, a tax-preparer is a person who prepares tax returns for clients at a stated fee. Suppose now you have no set fees—that you merely accept gifts or gratuities; and that, instead of putting pen to paper, you merely instruct your clients how to do so. Are you then a tax-preparer within the meaning of the law? I think not."

Thereafter, he did not write a word on any form. He did not sign the return, much less enter his Social Security number on it. He did not retain a copy of the report or keep a list of his "clients."

When a return was completed, the two friends shook hands, and the taxpayer left a gratuity on the desk—usually a $20 federal reserve note for ordinary returns. When more elaborate computations were involved, taxpayers made larger donations.

In several instances, they learned so much about income-tax procedures that in the future they were able to make out their our reports.

# *IRS Is Stymied*

In 1979 the IRS issued an extensive "manual supplement," describing 11 techniques commonly used by tax resisters to avoid or evade U.S. income taxation.

However, this did not even mention the three most common and important forms:

- Not filing any returns at all;
- Underreporting, especially by the self-employed; and
- The underground economy.

Both Congress and the IRS became acutely aware of these, and in September the House Subcommittee on Commerce, Consumer and Monetary Affairs held hearings.

Among other statements, Jerome Kurtz, commissioner of internal revenue, declared that only 60 to 64 percent of self-employment income is reported. He continued:

"We anticipate a backlog of 700,000 uncompleted nonfiler investigations by the end of 1980, and we must select those cases to which we will devote our limited resources.

"Nonfilers are difficult and expensive to deal with . . . Our report shows that unreported income from self-employment is a problem area . . . Self-employed noncompliers are difficult to identify and costly to audit . . . The self-employment 'gap' ranges from $33 to $100 billion . . . Noncompliance by independent contractors is widespead. At least 47 percent of such workers reported none of their compensation for income-tax purposes.

"Social Security tax compliance is even worse. About 62 percent paid none of the Social Security taxes due . . .

"Over one-third of the workers with adjusted gross incomes between $15,000 and $20,000 failed to report any of their compensation for income-tax purposes, and over 50 percent failed to pay Social Security tax . . ."

On the following day, Richard Folger, associate director of the General Accounting Office, stated that there was underground income of "at least $135 billion, on which taxes are not paid . . ." He stated further that it is impossible to determine the extent of lost revenue, because that of non-filers is not even considered in making estimates of treasury losses.

The IRS has been unsuccessful in determining where fraud exists or what its extent may be. Most "underreporters are not pursued and some are not even identified . . . IRS does not know how many underreporters, or how much unreported income," there may be.

Howard J. Hoffman, in a prepared statement, declared that the IRS needs a large sum of money to study the underground economy; that Congress should extend withholding to all forms of income; that steps must be taken to uncover the underground economy, for, at the present time, the "service" is simply swamped and cannot possibly handle this staggering job.

Since it does not know the extent of the rebellion and does not have the manpower to identify and pursue even the tax-cheaters IRS is certain exist, millions are now evading untold billions of taxes. Of at least 5 million non-filers, fewer than 600,000 can even be investigated. The 1980 backlog was at least 700,000 incomplete investigations.

Even after the IRS identifies "evaders" and assesses deficiencies against them, it will be difficult to collect any of the "money due" from them.

The official IRS "Report" dated September 1, 1979, declares in part:

● Protesting nonfilers and stop-filers are very difficult to identify and their number remains unknown.

● Under existing conditions, the "service" is simply unable to determine the scope of "illegal" tax-resistance or how many nonfilers or stop-filers there may be.

● There is a growing "abuse" of Form W-4; for example, several thousand employees of a single corporation were found to have filed false forms, claiming an excessive number of exemptions and allowances.

● In several states, employees filed suits against employers who refuse to accept the allowances listed on Form W-4.

Employers have no real incentive to inform the IRS of W-4 Form "abuses."

● "Illegal churches" have proliferated and often they are difficult to identify.

● A great many people have taken an "illegal" vow of poverty, but these also are difficult to identify; and it is expensive to assess and attempt to collect taxes from them.

● "IRS employees have become frustrated by illegal tax protestors directing unwarranted criticism against them, harassing them at work and at home and conducting character assassinations through various publications. Potential exists for physical attack on IRS employees dealing with illegal tax protestors since they are not always initially identified as such and employees may not take prudent precautions . . .

"In certain parts of the country—rural areas more than urban—violent protest has occurred. In many of those situations a seizure of property for non-payment of taxes has evoked threats and assaults . . .

"Frequently, illegal tax protestors will have a group of five to 20 persons accompany them to an IRS office. They will use the same tactic if an IRS representative has scheduled an appointment at their residences or places of business.

"During these confrontations, the IRS representative is often berated and verbally abused. In some instances, veiled threats have been made against them and their families . . . Harassment has continued through telephone calls . . . at work and at home . . ."

But listen to this: "The request to tape record the examination is a common delaying tactic . . . To remove this . . . and provide uniformity in protest cases, recording equipment should be available in all posts of duty, and the taxpayer should be allowed to record, as long as the service makes its own recording at the same time."

At least this is something. From now on, no taxpayer or individual being subjected to an audit or an examination should permit this to proceed without the use of tape recorders. Here, in addition to various court decisions, is IRS authority for such procedure.

# Put IRS Audit on Tape

A very sensitive question that often arises during an IRS audit is the use of tape recorders by taxpayers. Although there is no provision in the IR code nor in any regulation which bans or questions the use of such a device, the agency is "paranoid" concerning them. A statement in the "IRS Manual" purports to limit their use, but this does not have the force of law.

When asked why the bureau objects, agents may reply that tape recorders "interfere with the free interchange of ideas"—which is perhaps the silliest reason that could possibly be offered.

The fact is, of course, that agents are normally guilty of so much misrepresentation and outright lying that they are terrified of having their words in a permanent record, and one which cannot be denied. You can be certain that when audits take place at IRS headquarters, hidden microphones are installed there.

I have suggested that every taxpayer have not one, but TWO recorders in place and in operation whenever he engages an IRS agent in a conference at his home or office. He should, of course, also have live witnesses present, as is authorized in "Publication 556." He is completely within his rights if he refuses to submit to any kind of audit without these. If the agent insists, he should be offered the tape from one of the recorders. If he refuses to conduct the conference with a recorder, that should signal the summary end of the discussion.

Not only is there no law prohibiting the use of recorders: the courts have sanctioned them. In a Spokane, Wash., case a federal district judge ordered the IRS to permit a taxpayer to record, provided the agency received a tape. Unfortunately, I have not been able to obtain the date or the number of the case or the name of the judge. However, on Oct. 2, 1978, in the U.S. District Court of Arizona, Civil # 78-687, a similar case, came up before Walter E. Craig, chief federal district judge in the state (a former president of the American Bar Association). He declared that if the IRS agent is permitted to tape a conversation during an audit or hearing, the taxpayer must be allowed the same right. The transcript of this hearing is available, and I suggest that every person interested in this matter obtain a copy of it and have it on hand whenever he entertains any IRS personnel in his home or office, or even when he is interviewed at IRS headquarters.

No taxpayer can legally be denied the privilege of recording any conversation he has with IRS personnel. I repeat, therefore, that he should have TWO recorders—as well as several witnesses—with him whenever an audit occurs.

# Capital Gains Taxes on Sales

There is a little-known but very important provision in the Internal Revenue Code which the IRS does not publicize. It can save taxpayers thousands of dollars when they sell depreciable property, such as rental housing, a warehouse, shopping center or even machinery or other equipment. The code provides that if 30 percent or more of a depreciable asset is received during the first year of sale, the entire capital-gains tax falls due at once. But if the amount received is less than 30 percent, only the portion which is capital gain is taxable.

Thus, if a property which cost $60,000 is sold for $100,000 with a down payment of $25,000, two-fifths or 40 percent of the $25,000 might be reportable as income; *but this would be the case only if this payment exceeded the undepreciated remainder of the investment.*

No tax is due until the seller has recovered the undepreciated portion of the investment, known as the *basis.* In the above case, the land, which is never depreciated, may have been set up in the owner's books at $10,000; and the building at $50,000, which, after 10 years of operation, may have been depreciated to $25,000. The remainder, or basis, is then $35,000. Until this has been recovered, no tax is due. The $25,000 received in the year of sale is therefore nontaxable; and no tax will be due until the debt of the buyer has been reduced to $65,000.

Of course, any interest received will be taxable as ordinary, current income.

Whenever the payments the buyer makes to the seller reduce the unpaid balance below $65,000, any such reduction will be reportable and taxable. Thus, if during the third year of the contract or trust agreement, the balance is reduced from $65,000 to $60,000, there will be $5,000 of taxable income. But only 40 percent of this, or $2,000, is reportable and taxable as ordinary income in addition, of course, to interest.

It is of the utmost importance that taxpayers understand this. Publication 544, entitled "Sales and Other Dispositions of Assets," has a great deal of information. But nowhere does it explain that no tax is due on the sale of depreciable property (or, in fact, any other kind) until the basis or undepreciated portion of the investment has been recovered.

Therefore, if the IRS attempts to collect taxes on partial payments before the entire basis has been recovered, they are bluffing. For example, in the above case, they might declare incorrectly that a portion of the down payment is subject to taxation.

Also, because capital gains are listed as preference income, the piggyback tax of 15 percent does not apply until such annual gain exceeds $10,000. If accelerated depreciation has been taken on real estate, the IR Code provides that a recovery tax can be imposed following a sale. But, this does not apply after 10 years of operation, no matter what the acceleration has been.

# Capital Gains Taxes on Contracts

My article of June 25, 1980 stated that no capital gains tax is due on the sale of depreciable property until the actual investment or undepreciated basis has been fully recovered. Afterward I received a spate of inquiries on the subject.

As I said in that article, IRS "Publication 544" discusses in great detail the question of tax involved in the sale of property. But it does not explain all the facts; nor does the code itself explicitly say that no capital-gains tax is due until the basis has been recovered.

The fact is, such immunity exists by interpretation and regulation and is derived primarily from Sec. 453.

I became vitally interested in this matter about a year ago and called the IRS for clarification. I was told that "since there is case law on both sides" of this question, it is "uncertain" whether a tax could be imposed on capital gains before complete recovery of basis. But they could cite no unfavorable case law; I know now that none exists.

The "Master Tax Guide" (Commerce Clearing House, 4025 W. Peterson Ave., Chicago, Ill. 60646) is at least as authoritative as the code itself, with most valuable material. In the 1978 edition we find:

● There is no recapture of accelerated depreciation after 10 years of operation (Par. 988).

● The contract price to a seller of real estate or other property is what he actually receives—not the amount paid by the buyer, from which is subtracted realtor's commissions, escrow fees, title insurance charges, etc (Par. 667).

● "A cash basis seller who does not receive the purchase price in the year of sale, either in cash, notes, or other negotiable obligations which are the same as cash, does not report any gain until he has fully recovered his adjusted basis for the property sold" (Par. 999). The authority on which this is based is not contained in the code itself, but is spelled out in the 1978 "Standard Federal Tax Reports" (available in any good law library), in Secs. 2831.063 and 2874.01. Sec. 2831.063 says:

**If the obligations of the purchaser have no readily realizable market value, gain or profit to the cash-basis taxpayer will thereafter arise only when the amount realized upon the obligations exceeds the cost to the taxpayer of the property sold, after reduction by the amount of prior payment . . .**

**Where a cash-basis taxpayer sells property on contract, receiving a down payment in cash, and the vendee's contractual obligation (but not evidenced by purchase money notes) to pay the balance of the purchase price is in deferred payments extending over a period of years, he ordinarily will not immediately realize any gain.**

**The "recovery of cost" approach will apply, that is, all payments on principal will be credited against seller's basis until it is reduced to zero and then all payments will be reported as gain. The reason this procedure applies is because under such circumstances the vendee's contractual obligation is not considered the equivalent of cash, and therefore the only amount realized by him in the year the sale on contract is executed is the sum of cash received.**

## Sec. 2874.01 says:

**If a sale is made on contract, not secured by a negotiable note or mortgage, the Tax Court has repeatedly held that the cash-basis seller realizes no taxable gain until the cash collections under the contract exceed his basis.**

There is no other law or authority—and if the IRS tells you otherwise, they are ignorant, or bluffing and lying.

# *Going on Contract*

The Revenue Act of 1978 contains the best news for independent contractors that has ever emanated from Capitol Hill. This new law makes it far easier than ever before for an employee to attain the status of an independent contractor, which means that his employer will not deduct and transmit to the IRS either Social Security or income tax payments; nor will there be other deductions, such as union dues, insurance fees, etc. In short, the independent contractor receives the entire amount for which he works, and then makes his own reports and pays his own taxes on whatever amounts he divulges.

Since the independent contractor cannot be closely policed nor can his income be determined with accuracy, the IRS has made it as difficult as possible for workers to achieve this status. It has declared that unless such individuals maintain their own offices, offer their services to the general public, work for more than one employer, make all their own reports promptly and use their own tools and equipment, they cannot qualify.

However, under the new law, it is much easier to qualify, and the IRS cannot interfere with or question such employee-employer relationship.

A new section (530) has been added to the code, entitled "Controversies Involving Whether Individuals are Employees for Purposes of the Employment Taxes." This provides that:

"If for purposes of employment taxes, the taxpayer did not treat an individual as an employee for any period ending before Jan. 1, 1980, and in the case of periods after Dec. 31, 1978, all federal tax returns (including information returns) required for such periods are filed on a basis consistent with the taxpayer's treatment of such individual as not being an employee, then, for purposes of applying such taxes for such period with respect to the taxpayer, the individual shall be deemed not to be an employee . . . ."

The only requirement, under Sec. 530 (a) (3), is that such treatment be consistent with that accorded others.

In short, if an employer treats one who works for him as an independent contractor—consistently with treatment given others—during the year 1979, then such worker shall be given the status of independent contractor; and the section goes on to declare that "no regulation or revenue ruling shall be published on or after the date of the enactment of this act and before Jan. 1, 1980 . . . by the Department of the Treasury (including the Internal Revenue Service) with respect to the employment status of any individual for purposes of the employment taxes."

Thus, a person is treated as an independent contractor by the person for whom he performs work or service of any kind in the future if such treatment has already been established and if the individual files his own required reports with the IRS. And the IRS is prohibited from issuing any ruling or regulation which might invalidate such relationship.

Sec. 501 of the IR Code now provides that employees are no longer required to make any disclosure to their employers concerning any tips they receive directly.

# Resisting IRS Pressures

Unless an IRS agent can bring in at least $100 for every hour spent in auditing, he is not worth his salt.

He is therefore trained to employ every trick known in the realm of sophistry, make illegal assessments, hoping that, because of ignorance, loss of time, cost of defense, etc., taxpayers will agree to make whatever payment is demanded and thus close the case.

When the taxpayer yields to such pressure, he becomes the ideal prey for future extortion; and it is not only his patriotic duty to resist, but also the road to self-preservation.

If every taxpayer would pursue the methods we now suggest, the IRS would soon be shorn of its dictatorial power:

• When it makes an assessment by disallowing valid deductions or uses some alleged but unknown regulation or provision to increase tax liability, the taxpayer should pursue every administrative device available. He should remember that more often than otherwise, in order to please his superiors, the agent is attempting to bulldoze his victim into making excessive payments.

• Even if the assessment believed to be invalid is only $10, this should be resisted by every means possible. **Do not be defeated.**

• The taxpayer should obtain a copy of the IRS Code from Prentice-Hall or the Commerce Clearing House, which also publishes a Master Tax Guide, a very useful document.

• The taxpayer should study carefully the provisions of the code to discover whether those on which the agent bases his authority to assess an additional tax are subject to interpretation. They may actually mean the opposite of what he says.

• He should then demand a conference at the District level, where he can dispute and resist every IRS contention. He should obtain a copy of IRS "Publication 556," which outlines the appeal rights available to every taxpayer.

• If the conferee upholds the agent's findings (as he usually does) the taxpayer should demand a hearing at the appellate level, where careful preparation will be necessary, including a well-written brief, based on a study of the code and court decisions.

In this procedure, the taxpayer should consult the monumental "U.S. Code Annotated, Title 26," published by the West Publishing Co. and available in good law libraries everywhere. It lists every court decision of record pertaining to all sections and subsections of the code.

• If satisfaction is not obtained at the appellate level, the taxpayer can go to the U.S. Tax Court, which, even though set up in the IRS code, claims to be completely independent of the IRS.

This is a court of record and cases argued there require considerable preparation. However, taxpayers can do their own work even here by studying the "Rules of Practice and Procedure," which can be obtained from the Government Printing Office for $1.10 or from the U.S. Tax Court.

• If millions of Americans would appeal their cases in this manner, it would be years before they could even be heard; the administrative machinery of the IRS would become clogged beyond operational possibility.

Through such appeals, furthermore, millions of Americans would obtain a valuable education, and the shock troops necessary to bring the monster under control sometimes referred to as the Infernal Revenue Stripper would be created.

# The IRS: Its Impossible Task

It is always appropriate to offer some suggestions as to what a citizen should do if he receives a message from IRS that he is to be investigated or audited.

Consider the situation of a person who has not filed a return and does not intend to do so.

In 1975, 101 million persons in the U.S. were subject to Social Security payments or withholding. However, there were only 82,177,000 income-tax returns, and of these only 61,753,000 paid any tax. In other words, there were 20,424,000 returns which reported income but no tax-liability. However, in that year more than 100 million persons were subject to the Social Security tax; of these, therefore, some 18 million made no return whatever and nearly 40 million paid no income tax.

Obviously more and more Americans are joining the ranks of the non-payers and non-filers. No doubt millions are neither paying nor reporting their incomes. Millions of others are drastically underreporting them.

The extent and nature of this rebellion is such that the IRS cannot cope with it. The agency has neither the manpower nor the facilities to investigate millions of dropouts. We have no doubt that, right now, great numbers of wage-workers are either writing "exempt" on Line 3 of the W4 Form, or taking a sufficient number of exemptions and allowances thereon so that no refund will be due if a return is filed. Since they have no expectation of receiving any refund, they are simply "forgetting" to file a return.

When such persons receive form-letters demanding a return, many simply throw them into the wastebasket. Some have been known to write "deceased" or "moved—left no address" on the envelope and return it. What can the IRS do when such mail is returned?

If and when an IRS agent telephones proposing an audit, or shows up unexpectedly at an individual's home or office, he will be told that all communications must be by letter and that no conversation will take place. This citizen may be one of the many millions who owe no tax and who are not even required to file a return.

The IRS does not know in what category a person belongs if he has not filed a return. In 1979, a wage-earner with a wife and six children is not required to file unless his income exceeds $11,400. If he refuses to answer questions or enter into any discussion with the IRS agent, the agency will be forced to discover through its own research anything it is to know.

In summary, tax-resisters and dropouts do not communicate with the IRS—at least not until they have been indicted, arrested, and charged with income-tax evasion.

# Illegal IRS Threats

I remember as if it were yesterday the occasion in 1946 when I was ordered to appear at IRS headquarters in Detroit with all my books and records—which they kept for 18 months. Although I had paid all taxes conscientiously, an agent began the conversation by stating that they "knew" I had evaded $45,000 due; and that, therefore, everything I owned would be confiscated and that I would be placed behind prison bars. To obtain the information they needed, I was ordered to prepare the notorious Ten-Year-Net-Worth Statement.

Today, no one can be forced to appear at an IRS office with books and records without a court order; the agency is not empowered to keep these if it obtains them, or even to copy any of them or remove them from a taxpayer's home or office; it may look at those for any year only once; if it wants a Net-Worth Statement, the IRS must prepare it on the basis of its own research. And now the secret "Official IRS Tax Audit Guide" sternly warns agents never to threaten or attempt to intimidate a taxpayer. However, if they feel safe in so doing, they still indulge in this despicable practice.

I recently learned of a case in which an agent did so with a well-known woman who had a hidden tape recorder in operation. He pointed to her piano, furniture, car and other possessions. "We are going to take all these," he declared, "and put a lien on your house and seize your bank accounts."

She invited him to expand on his theme, which he did, until it seemed nothing would survive the imminent assessment. Thinking that he had sufficiently put the fear of Big Brother into her heart, the agent left, no doubt with a feeling of exuberant joy. (You must understand, of course, that there had been no proof of fraud or underpayment in respect to this taxpayer.)

This woman thereupon went to Washington, where she related the whole incident to her representative and her two senators. With letters from them in her pocket, she called upon a high IRS official, who summoned the agent for an explanation. After he had emphatically denied her version of what happened, she played the tape.

The agent was fired.

No wonder IRS personnel hate and fear tape recorders. No wonder they dislike witnesses and even try to bluff taxpayers by saying that they may not be present at a conference, even though "Publication 556" states explicitly, they may not only attend, but may even speak for the taxpayer.

I have known others who had concealed tape recorders in operation during conversations with IRS agents; and I suggest that if, during such a conference, the agent makes any improper statement—whether it be of a threatening or intimidating nature, or simply misleading or incorrect—the resulting tape be used to the hilt in order to bring down upon such agent the full penalties now available for the protection of the taxpayer.

# Fifth Amendment Immunity

I have received a spate of mail asking whether it is safe or desirable to file- the Fifth-Amendment return.

This is not a simple question. But, I would say that if the person making such a return has no traceable income or any property readily seizable, there is little the IRS can do in retaliation. This is essentially the technique used by Austin Flett for 14 years while he traveled up and down the country lambasting the IRS and the federal government. He must have had a considerable income, for he declared that he spent $200,000 during his crusade but never paid a penny of tax.

Many have placed their property beyond reach of the IRS by establishing irrevocable trusts; by having no bank accounts; by placing real estate in other names; by leasing cars etc. This is what Dr. E.A. Cupp of Uniontown, Pennsylvania, has been doing for years, while he continues his professional work. He wrote recently that the IRS now says he owes $150,000, but that he will never, never pay one penny of this.

In its "Manual Supplement" of January 10, 1979, the IRS listed 11 methods by which tax rebels are resisting. One of these is the Fifth Amendment return. When the agency receives one of these, it normally sends a form letter stating that it is not acceptable; that in the "Porth case," the Supreme Court so declared; and it then includes a copy of Sec. 7203 of the IRS Code, which provides that returns containing complete information are required.

However, there is more to be said: Several Supreme Court decisions, notably "Garner," state explicitly that if any information on a return might incriminate or tend to do so, such information is not required. "Garner" goes further: It declares that if a citizen's income derives from criminal sources entirely, no return at all is necessary. In that case, the IRS could conduct only a civil action and determine tax liability on the basis of its own independent research.

This does not mean that non-criminals may never make Fifth-Admendment returns without danger of conviction. Norbert Stelton in Minnesota and Charles Riely in Arizona were acquitted on charges of not filing proper returns; and Charles Rietz of California had two hung juries in Fifth-Amendment cases.

However, others have been convicted; and, in any event, such procedures are difficult, time-consuming and costly. Furthermore, even though these stalwarts were victorious, the IRS could still make civil assessments and seize unprotected property.

Marvin Cooley, who was convicted several years ago, later adopted a much more sophisticated defense based entirely on the Fifth Amendment; and he is on a constant crusade somewhat similar to, but far more advanced than, that of Austin Flett. Every year, he files a Fifth-Amendment return, and the IRS does nothing whatsoever about it, although everyone knows that he has a substantial but untraceable income.

Finally, we should note that whereas the IRS admits that it has received hundreds of Fifth-Amendment returns (the actual number is probably in the thousands or tens of thousands), it has prosecuted only a few vocal leaders; it is simply too costly and time-consuming to do otherwise.

Whether the Fifth-Amendment return is suitable or desirable for any individual is a matter that each must decide for himself.

# Bluff and Deceit

As the tax returns become more complicated and confusing, audits require more time, and the Internal Revenue Service (IRS) does not have the manpower to handle as many as it would like, in the necessary detail. Remember also these facts:

- If the IRS calls to say it wants to audit your return, tell it that all communications must be in writing;

- You have the right to postpone the meeting a reasonable number of times;

- You do not have to go to an IRS office, unless you wish to do so, for it is your right to have a conference at a time and place convenient for you;

- The IRS may never examine the same records more than once;

- It cannot force you to show anything which is already in its possession;

- It may neither copy nor remove any record in your possession;

- You have a right to have witnesses present at any interview, who may also speak for you without identifying themselves;

- You have a right to use a tape recorder, provided only that the agent has the use of one also; and finally,

- Don't make it too easy for an agent, because it is extremely important to him that he complete your audit as quickly as possible—his time is very valuable indeed.

We note that in 1979, the IRS audited 2.11 percent of all individual returns; in 1980, 2.02 percent; but in 1981, only 1.77 percent. If you do not itemize—i.e., if you use only the zero deduction—your chances of being picked for audit are much reduced, unless, perhaps, you have a business which claims a large operating loss.

One of the significant changes in the Tax Equity and Fiscal Responsibility Act of 1982 provides that restaurants with more than 10 employees must report their total sales so that the amounts supposedly allocated to each waiter or waitress can be estimated. The restaurant will then compute the business done by each and estimate his tips at 8 percent of the bills. The IRS will assess deficiencies if this amount is not reported.

Stockbrokers are now required to report all sales of securities. (The Act required banks and savings and loan associations to withhold income taxes on interest payments; but this was repealed in 1983.)

Remember that if you have itemized deductions and IRS audits your return, it will disallow these and recompute your tax liability unless you verify them. So be sure to keep receipts, canceled checks, and other supporting documentation for at least three years.

## IN CASE OF AUDIT

In case of an audit, never volunteer any information to an agent. Answer only what is absolutely necessary. Be firm and polite, not hostile or over-friendly. Never agree to a deficiency or sign such an agreement unless you are absolutely certain that the tax is due and cannot be avoided.

If you receive a letter stating that you

owe more taxes because of an error, do not send any money until you receive a full and convincing explanation.

I have known a number of cases in which the IRS has collected money not due by sheer bluff and deceit.

If you receive an unexplained refund, just cash your check and forget it.

The IRS declares that in 1981, it lost $87.2 billion because of underpayments by individuals alone. And this does not include the millions of "dropouts," who made no returns at all. So you see that the agency really has its hands full and cannot now, or ever, hope to cope fully with the problem. Clever and careful people by the millions—possibly tens of millions—are avoiding considerable portions or all of their federal and state income taxes.

If you do not agree with an agent's findings, never sign a consent agreement, for then you lose all rights of appeal. You can dispute them in the district office. If you are not satisfied with the results there, you can proceed to the appellate level, and, from there, to the tax court, where it might take years to hear your case—and where, as an average, disputes are settled at a much lower figure than the agent who is very anxious to make a good showing by assessing the largest possible deficiencies, demanded originally.

**CONFRONTATION**

In my last confrontation with the IRS, more than 20 years ago, the agent declared that I owed $24,000. However, I ended up paying nothing at all, and collecting $38,500 from them which I would not have known was due me except for the battle which covered almost two years. This is one instance of what can happen if you are ready, willing and able to take on the agency in earnest. Had I at that time had at my disposal a manual such as "How to Defend Yourself Against the IRS,"* my victory would have come much more easily.

Some more tips to remember: Anyone working for a wage or a salary can now establish his own individual retirement account (IRA) with maximum deductible payments of $2,000 a year—which, at 8 percent interest, will grow to $166,200 in 25 years. At 12 percent, an investment of $84,000 will become $1,920,000 in 42 years.

A joint spousal account may invest $2,250 annually, tax deductible. Or, if both work, each can have one with $2,000 annual payments.

Keogh accounts for self-employed individuals can be much larger: 15 percent of adjusted gross income with a maximum of $15,000 annually. Such an investment made annually for 40 years at 12 percent interest will become $16,877,636. Remember that no tax on this will be due until benefits are withdrawn after retirement.

If a person retires from employment at, say, the age of 65 with a lump-sum pension payment of $110,000, this can be invested without tax in an IRA rollover account, which—at 12 percent interest—will grow to $228,261 by the age of mandatory retirement, which is 70½. He can then draw the entire amount due him in installments over a 12-year period—with much smaller tax liability. And these will total no less than $486,062.

These are only a few of the important points which may be utilized to the advantage of millions of American taxpayers. I suggest that everyone who can do so to the utmost.

---

*"How to Defend Yourself Against the IRS" is available for $175.00 from Government Educational Foundation, Box 1622, Washington, D.C. 20013. Payment for this loose-leaf manual includes future updates as they are issued.

# *Agents' Handbook*

About two years ago, I wrote an article concerning the secret Internal Revenue Service (IRS) "Handbook for Special Intelligence Agents." At one time this was limited strictly to officials in the service; however, under the Freedom of Information Act, the IRS was forced to supply this material to taxpayers upon proper demand.

Formerly it was obtainable at very reasonable cost but now the price has soared to $75.90. It is printed on both sides of very thin paper and is difficult to read. Furthermore, the new editions of the work contain very little important or useful information for taxpayers, such as is found in earlier editions and which may be used by taxpayers in their defense.

Actually, I received two versions issued on the same date in 1983 but quite different from each other, but neither of much value to taxpayers. However, all the provisions in previous editions are still valid.

I have therefore reproduced the valuable portions of the 1982 edition together with some portions of the 1983 versions in an easily readable format. The document contains 400 pages, printed on one side of heavy white paper.

In addition to the index provided in the text—which is difficult to decipher—I have supplied another, which pinpoints the important elements of the "Handbook"—provisions that the IRS normally will not reveal, but which the taxpayer can force the service to obey if he knows of their existence.

In addition to much else, I have reproduced materials explaining the following:

1) The statute of limitations for civil audits and criminal prosecutions;

2) The rules and regulations concerning evidence;

3) Where and when the burden of proof is on the government;

4) The rules concerning, and the functions of, informers;

5) Procedures IRS must follow in obtaining bank records;

6) Rules which protect taxpayers from IRS when seeking to examine the contents of safety boxes;

7) Protection provided by the Fourth and Fifth Amendments;

8) Inadmissibility of evidence obtained illegally by IRS;

9) Restrictions in the use of surveillance;

10) Right of taxpayers to record interviews with the IRS;

11) Right of taxpayers to take the Fifth Amendment;

12) Books and records may be obtained only by voluntary consent;

13) IRS requirement to give the Miranda warning;

14) What constitutes voluntary waiver of Constitutional rights;

15) Information obtained by IRS thru trickery may not be used;

16) Absolute right of taxpayer to counsel;

17) Partnerships and associations have same rights as individuals;

18) Attorney-client, husband-wife, clergyman-penitent and physician-patient privilege;

19) Rules concerning confessions;

20) How agents are to conduct themselves during interviews;

21) Taxpayer must be given receipt for all records surrendered voluntarily; none may be copied or removed without taxpayer consent;

22) No "fishing expeditions" permissible;

23) Only one examination may be made of records for any one year;

24) Protection of records in hands of third parties;

25) Protection of churches against examination of books and records;

26) Fees and costs of witnesses and taxpayers which IRS must pay;

27) Rules concerning summonses;

28) Restrictions governing undercover work;

29) Unreasonable searches and seizures defined;

30) Rules regarding storage of seized personal property;

31) No law against telling people to make no return at all;

32) Statute of limitations means absolute amnesty;

33) Elements necessary to constitute conspiracy;

34) Legal defenses against charge of willfulness;

35) What constitutes entrapment—which is illegal;

36) In net worth investigation, burden of proof is on IRS to prove income taxable, and not exempt;

37) Voluntary statements in such investigation may be used against taxpayer;

38) Common defenses in such investigations—which must be conducted by IRS independently;

39) Definition and description of perjury;

40) Court jurisdiction limited by Constitution;

41) Rules governing grand jury hearings;

42) The expert witness rule;

43) Payments to be made to third parties for producing records;

44) The rights of corporation officers;

45) Rules regarding time and place of audits—must be convenient for taxpayers;

46) Witness fees and expenses; and

47) Rules concerning seizure of personal property—how to be stored.

This "Handbook,"* together with the manual, "How to Defend Yourself Against the IRS,"** constitute, to my knowledge, the best means of protection for taxpayers during audits. ␢

---

*"Handbook for Special Intelligence Agents" is available for $25 from Dr. Martin A. Larson, Box 15059, Phoenix, Ariz. 85060.

**"How to Defend Yourself Against the IRS" is available for $175.00 from Government Educational Foundation, Box 1622, Washington, D.C. 20013. Price includes all supplements issued for three years from date of order.

# Obtaining an IRS Ruling

For years, I have been trying to obtain a statement from the IRS concerning the taxability of a certain transaction which I consummated in 1958 and in which a high-priced lawyer sided with the IRS in stating that I owed money. Since then I have become absolutely certain that no tax was due. Again and again, I have attempted to obtain a definite statement from the IRS in regard to a transaction of this kind: but all I receive is double-talk with no specific reply.

I recently received a packet from IRS headquarters which describes the procedure which must be followed in order to obtain a ruling. As of November 1, 1976, new requirements were established, which must be met whenever requests for rulings and determinations are made. In addition to all information and material previously required, any taxpayer must now submit:

(1) A separate statement explaining the precise situation involved.

(2) A copy of all other submissions made by the taxpayer; and

(3) A declaration signed in the following form: "Under penalties of perjury, I have examined this request, including the accompanying documents, and to the best of my knowledge and belief, the facts presented in support of the requested ruling or determination are true, correct, and complete."

If the request does not include all such information, "the Service will notify the requester of the failure to comply with such requirements. If the taxpayer does not submit the requested material within 30 days after notification, the case will be closed."

In short, every request for information must deal with a specific and personal situation; and the IRS will not issue any ruling of a general nature which will serve to clarify the real meaning or intent of any provision in the Internal Revenue Code; it will leave this to the discretion of every agent in the field, who can therefore assess any doubtful or illegal deficiency he may wish. The taxpayer will then be compelled, at great expense and loss of time, to carry his case to the Appellate level, the Tax Court, and even to the Circuit Court of Appeals, where he may finally after years of battle, be victorious. And even so, the IRS never regards a defeat in such courts of precedential authority: each case is an individual dispute to be resolved separately.

It should be noted that even if a taxpayer is able to obtain a ruling and determination in his own particular case, it may be too late to do him any good; nor is there any certainty that the ruling will be in accord with law or equity, or that it will stand objective judicial scrutiny.

In this respect, we may mention the 8-year battle which raged between Phil and Sue Long of Bellevue, Washington, and the IRS, which assessed against them a liability exceeding $42,000 in 1969. This was upheld by the Appellate Division and by the Tax Court. Finally, however, in January, 1977, the Ninth Circuit Court of Appeals awarded a complete victory to the Longs, who now do not owe one penny of a liability which otherwise, including interest, would probably have approached $60,000. We should note that the Longs did practically all their own work and prepared their own briefs without the aid of lawyers; and that they were instrumental in prying loose from the IRS almost a truckload of formerly secret indoctrinational material, some of which was published a few years ago by the Church of Scientology under the title **The IRS Papers***. Almost all of their expenses, totaling some $20,000 or $25,000, were incurred for travel and the insertion of a series of articles in Washington newspapers called "Life Under the IRS in the United States."

*Available from Church of Scientology, 4833 Fountain Ave., Los Angeles, Calif. 90029

# Ch. 4

# Dividends, Deductions, and Dollars

# *Tax Reform Act of 1969*

The Tax Reform Act of 1969 created, as an adjunct of the Tax Court, a new division known as the small claims court, in which cases involving less than $5,000 in disputed taxes could be adjudicated. This court holds sessions in 120 cities, at least one in every state, where the taxpayer can, by paying a fee of $10, represent himself at an informal hearing.

The July 11, 1977 issue of "U.S. News & World Report" contains an article discussing the nature and operation of this tribunal. The number of cases it handled increased from 2,000 in 1972 to an estimated 3,040 in 1977.

Most cases are settled in pretrial conferences, in which the IRS may make concessions because no decision or compromise can ever be used as a precedent in another, or similar, dispute. In some cases, which do come to trial, the judge may prove somewhat sympathetic to the taxpayer if he seems completely sincere and honest.

However, we warn any person contemplating this route that there is no appeal from any decision in the Small Claims Court . . . and that the taxpayer going there may expect to be faced by tricky IRS attorneys who will use every method they can to defeat the appellant.

However, this Court does permit the taxpayer to present his own case and to do so without incurring heavy legal costs or great loss of time. If he is sure of his position and is certain that the IRS is using sheer bluff — as it so often does — he may win important points in pre-trial conferences without going to court at all.

However, if anyone is thinking of conducting his own defense in such a case, we advise him to:

• Obtain an exact Bill of Particulars from the IRS previous to any conference;
• Have in his possession up-to-date copies of the "Internal Revenue Code" and "The Master Tax Guide," published by the Commerce Clearing House, 4025 W. Peterson Ave., Chicago, Ill. 60646; and
• Study these carefully for information relating to his case before facing the IRS agents.

Marvellous are the things that countless taxpayers can learn by this method, among which is the fact that the IRS routinely demands money not due at all or more money than is due, under its own law.

One stunning victory over the IRS is the best thing that can happen in the life of an American citizen; for it will almost certainly guarantee that such citizen will thereafter be left studiously alone by the Great American Gestapo.

# Deductions Under the 1976 Tax Reform Act

For years, a great many people, probably millions, have been taking substantial income-tax deductions because they have used a portion of their homes for business purposes; most of these were school teachers or office employees, who perhaps had a small desk in a bedroom or some other portion of the house where certain papers were kept and where a certain amount of clerical work was alleged to be done in off hours at home.

The Tax Reform Act of 1976 has drastically tightened up its provisions dealing with this deduction. No allowance can now be taken because of business activity conducted by a taxpayer in the building which is also his residence unless a certain and definite portion of such building is set aside for the exclusive purpose of conducting his business and is his sole or at least his principal place of business.

This restriction will not, however, apply when a portion of the residence is used as a medical, dental, or real-estate office; or if the taxpayer has a money-earning occupation and a definite space in his home is set aside exclusively to earn such income. No one who works in an office or other place supplied by an employer can claim any portion of his home as a deductible business expense. The new law also provides that unless the business for which a deductible space in the home is used creates a gross income at least equal to the claimed exemption, no allowance will be made.

This means that if an author, cartoonist, public stenographer, consultant, etc., who has no other office, uses a specific portion of his home exclusively to carry on his activity and if this produces a gross—not necessarily a net—return, he may continue to report its value as a deduction from his Adjusted Gross Income. And it is not necessary that he itemize expenditures on the 1040 in order to claim it; he may include it as an item of expense in his Schedule C, Form 1040, profit (or loss) from business or profession.

The question then arises: How large a deduction can a qualified individual take? The IRS will generally try to limit such deduction to a ratio of the rent paid by the taxpayer or, if he is the owner, the actual cost of utilities and taxes paid.

Thus if one-sixth of the house is used for business, and if taxes, utilities, etc., total $1,200, the IRS may say that no more than $200 may be deducted, thus allowing nothing for depreciation or interest on investment. However, when they do so, they are bluffing: the taxpayer is entitled to take the full ratio of the rental value of the building. Thus, if the annual rent would be $4,800 and utilities and other expenses total $1,200, the taxpayer is entitled to one-sixth of $6,000, or $1,000; and if the IRS seeks to reduce this amount, the taxpayer should announce that he is prepared to carry the dispute to the Appellate Division or even to the Tax Court.

**(NOTE: Under a new law, a person who conducts a business not related to his regular employment may take a deduction for an office in his home.)**

# Keogh and IRA Retirement Plans

In our book, "The Great Tax Fraud," published in 1968, we advocated a system in which every person, self-employed or working for another, would be allowed to withdraw from Social Security on condition that he establish an irrevocable trust for himself, such as described in this column last week. Although the mills of the gods grind slowly, they do sometimes grind forward, if sufficient pressure is applied to them.

In 1964, Sec. 404(e), known as the Keogh Plan, had been added to the Internal Revenue Code. Under this, a self-employed individual could make tax-deductible contributions up to 10 per cent of his adjusted gross income, but not in excess of $2,500 a year, to his individual trust account with benefits available at age 59½, but not later than 70½.

This was a step in the right direction and we so described it. However, it did not go far enough; the maximum deduction was too small and the victim still could not escape the Social Security trap.

Then, effective Jan. 1, 1974, the Keogh Plan was expanded and permitted non-taxable contributions up to 15 per cent of AGI, but not to exceed $7,500 for the self-employed. However, there was still no escape from Social Security.

On Jan. 1, 1975, a more important section was added to the Code: 219, which provides that any employee not already covered by an annuity plan may establish his own Individual Retirement Account (IRA) by making a non-taxable contribution not to exceed $1,500 or 15 per cent of his AGI to such a retirement trust.

Again, however, no escape was provided from the S.S. program.

We should note that another development of the greatest importance has been expanding rapidly during recent years. In 1940, Private Pension and Profit-Sharing Plans covered 4.1 million persons; in 1973, 29 million. In the meantime, contributions increased from $380 million to $21 billion; benefits from $140 million to $11.2 billion; and reserves from $2.4 to an incredible $180 billion—totals which are constantly growing. By 1980, the reserves will probably exceed $250 billion.

In 1973, there were more than 178,000 private pension and profit-sharing plans. By 1980, it is projected that these will cover more than 42 million persons, far more than receive Social Security benefits.

In addition, private uninsured pension plans covered 7 million other employees, of whom 1,213,000 received $3.2 billion in benefits in 1972—an average of $2,675—considerably more than the average Social Security payment.

All this points the route by which this nation may place a period on the ill-fated Social Security experiment. The first step should consist in permitting any person, whether an employee or self-employed, to abandon the federal system by establishing his own mandatory and irrevocable trust account.

The second step would then consist in not only permitting, but requiring all the self-employed to do the same. The third and final step would then consist in terminating the federal program for everyone and requiring them to set up their own retirement trusts.

**(NOTE: Any employee may now deduct $2,000 as a contribution annually to his own IRA, which, in 40 years, would create a trust fund of more than $500,000. A self-employed person may contribute at a rate of 15 percent of AGI up to a maximum of $15,000 annually.)**

# *Employee Withholding Allowance Certificate*

Before 1972, the W-4 form, called the Employees Exemption Certificate, which everyone filed with employers, covered only dependants and included the perjury line, which made any misstatement a misdemeanor punishable by a year in prison and a fine of $500.

However, this was then changed to the Employees Withholding Allowance Certificate, which made provision for all deductions and carried no perjury provision.

Thus, in addition to exemptions for dependants, it provides equal allowances for interest, taxes, casualties, theft, accidents, medical expenses, charitable contributions, etc.

A married man with six children is allowed eight exemption allowances; if he pays real estate, sales, and other taxes totalling $1,500, he has two more allowances; if he gives $1,500 to his church and various charities, he is entitled to two more; if he has medical expenses of $2,250, he has three additional; if he pays $750 in interest, he has another; if he suffers $750 damage from flood, or windstorm, he has yet another; if his uninsured car is wrecked, he may have three more—for a total of 20 allowances, or $15,000, .

which is exempt from income taxation. On his certificate—the W-4, which he files with his employer—he will therefore claim this number, and on the portion he retains for himself, he will list eight allowances on lines (a), (b), and (g) and 12 on line (j).

Since the W-4 is filed at the beginning of each taxable year, the taxpayer must, and is permitted to, estimate the number of his probable allowances.

We have known some who have claimed 99—which is likely to cause lifted eyebrows and may bring repercussions or retaliation. However, since no one can determine all possible or even probable exigencies, the taxpayer is quite within his legal rights in being somewhat generous in this matter: if he is certain of 12, he may well claim 15 with safety.

This will render much and in many cases all of his weekly or bi-weekly wage immune to deductions for income taxation; and the objective should in all cases be to claim at least as many allowances as will appear on the 1040.

We believe that millions of taxpayers are now declaring enough allowances to preclude any refund because of over-withholding, which, in past years, has sometimes been so great as to require the disbursement of $15 or $20 billion by the IRS.

(NOTE: Since the above article was written, each exemption and other allowance has been increased to $1,000. Also, the old Form W4-E has been discontinued and Line 3 on the new Form W-4 provides a place for claiming exemption against income-tax withholding.)

(Note also that since any exmployee may now file up to 14 allowances on his W-4 without questioning from the IRS or any serious difficulty, there is no reason now why there should be any over-withholding for anyone or any expectation of a refund for those who do file.)

# Who's Paying Taxes?

Paul Getty is reliably reported to have earned or received $70 million personal income in one year and paid an income tax of $6,000.

Ferdinand Lundberg in "The Rich and the Super-Rich" describes a man whose personal income was $19 million and paid less in income taxes than his chauffeur.

After Mrs. Delphine Dodge invested her $56 million and received an annual income of about $2 million, she was not even required to file a 1040; had she earned $600 as a washerwoman, she could have been sent to prison for a failure to do so.

In 1969, David Rockefeller, Chairman of the Board of the Chase Manhattan Bank, stated in testimony before the House Ways and Means Committee that although he did not owe any income tax, he nevertheless, out of the kindness of his heart, sent a small check each year to the IRS.

The favored individuals and corporations escape at least $70 billion of income taxes which they would have to pay, if they were to be assessed as are the incomes of the great, producing middle class.

The IRS Code, in addition to its exorbitant demands for money, is filled with provisions which, on the one hand, are designed to make the incomes of favored individuals and corporations immune wholly or largely to taxation; and, on the other, with traps and snares designed to destroy any honest, hard-working, and self-reliant individual who threatens, by his own efforts, to become sufficiently successful so that he can create a substantial estate for himself.

It thus becomes obvious that the primary purpose of the Internal Revenue Code and Service is not to collect taxes, but to regiment the people and create a caste-society, in which the producer-workers shall be reduced to perpetual servitude by being forced to maintain great hordes of parasitical idlers and, in addition, create the wealth by which the very rich become the perpetual super-rich.

Since those so highly privileged abhor any substantial addition to their numbers, they have created a system of income-taxation which not only protects their wealth and privileges but which also keeps the vast mass of productive citizens in subjection.

In order to prevent the flames of revolution from bursting around them, they have devised a system of welfare which costs them nothing but compels the useful workers to support millions of indigent parasites who, as a result, support the super-rich who, like the Kennedys, are always proposing vast welfare programs, the cost of which does not fall on them.

However, as the creators of wealth become more and more aware of how this system operates, they are filled with resentment and are attracted to the tax-rebellion, which is destined one day to result in a more equitable means of supporting a much smaller, but constitutional, federal government.

# *Our Foreign Profiteers*

Outrageous as are many of the immunities and inequities embedded in the Internal Revenue Code and conferred upon favored individuals and entities, Sections 892 and 895 certainly rank among the worst. Section 895 states that:

"Income derived by a foreign central bank of issue from obligations of the United States or any agency or instrumentality thereof and which are owned by such foreign central bank of issue, or derived from interest on deposits with persons carrying on the banking business, shall not be included in gross income and shall be exempt from taxation under this subtitle . . ."

Simply stated, this means, for example, that the potential profit to be made on the 18,000 tons of gold now lying in the vaults of the New York branch of the Federal Reserve System and earmarked to foreign ownership—that is, foreign banks of issue like the Reichsbank, the Banque de France, etc.—will not be subject either to taxation or disclosure. Since the gold was purchased at $35 an ounce, that profit would be about $300 billion if sold at $600 an ounce. It also means that such banks can hold unlimited amounts of federal securities and derive unlimited amounts of revenue from funds deposited in American banks without being subject either to taxation or disclosure.

Section 892 states that:

"The income of foreign governments or international organizations received from investments in the United States in stocks, bonds, or other domestic securities, owned by such foreign governments or by international organizations, or from interest on deposits in the United States of moneys belonging to such foreign government or international organization, or from any other source within the United States, shall not be included in gross income and shall be exempt from taxation under this title."

Simply stated, again, this means that any foreign government may derive unlimited, undisclosed, and untaxed income from any kind of investment in the United States. It means, for example, that the Panamanian government could use money to be given it under the treaties recently approved by the U.S. Senate for investments in the United States, the revenues from which would be immune to both disclosure and taxation.

However, this section of the code goes far beyond providing immunity for such governments: it extends to all "international organizations" also, which includes ecclesiastical and mercantile corporations. The only requirement is that they operate internationally—that is, in more than one country. A case in point is the Societa General Immobiliare, an Italian-based real-estate cartel, which has constructed projects in various countries, including the Watergate Apartments in Washington, on which its estimated untaxed and unreportable profits totalled about $50 million.

An interesting facet concerning Watergate is that when it was constructed, the Vatican owned controlling interest in the Societa; however, after the Italian parliament passed a law taxing the commercial revenues of the Vatican, it gradually divested itself of shares in Italian corporations; and we understand that much of its profits and investments have been transferred to American securities or deposits in American banks, where all revenues remain completely immune to taxation and disclosure.

# Who Gets the Gravy?

Whenever I criticize federal employees, I am sure to receive several letters from present or former such personnel, complaining that they are "short-changed." One, for example, declared that he is "worse off" than those on Social Security because, since he has long ago consumed his own contributions to his annuity, he must now pay income taxes on what he receives. SS retirees, he moans, are not under this obligation.

Such letters move me to make a few observations. In 1935, I opened a paint store in Detroit. I lived on a dollar a day in a room which I had constructed in the back of the store; worked 75 hours a week; and a few years later, paid enough in federal income taxes to support two full-time bureaucrats. If the government had been operating my business, I have no doubt that the annual operating deficit would have been at least $50,000.

Federal employees can leave the service at any time and receive in refund every penny they have contributed to their own retirement plan. Or they can retire at the end of 20 years with a very good pension or at 30 with one that is munificient.

For example, Sen. Barry Goldwater's (R-Ariz.) secretary, with a salary of $51,000, could retire after 24 years of service with an annuity of $27,000; or, if she is permitted to pay the $10,000 (including interest) to cover the four years she was out of the service, she could draw $31,000 for the rest of her life. This is more than $2,500 a month—not bad. Like all other federal employees, she has contributed 7 percent of her salary to her own retirement; but, at $31,000 a year, all this would soon be consumed.

A great many federal employees, still at the peak of their earning powers, leave the service with very generous pensions and immediately take other very-well-paying jobs, which, in due course, soon provides a second very generous annuity: a practice known as double-dipping.

For example, most of the judges and other highly paid officials in the U.S. Tax Court are former IRS employees now on federal pension. In bitter contrast, if those on Social Security try to leave the system, the government will seize their property and threaten them with prison terms.

In the case of Dr. James Owen of Portland, Oregon, the federal judge told the defendant that if he tried to quote the Constitution during his trial, he would be "guilty of contempt of court" and subject to indefinite imprisonment.

SS retirees are not eligible to receive regular benefits before 65; and if they earn more than a few dollars, their pay is subject to a 50 percent surtax. We should note also that more than 25 percent of all those who contribute to Social Security die before retirement and they receive nothing whatever for their multibillion-dollar contributions.

Those on SS collectively pay the entire cost of the system; the taxpayers contribute 80 percent of the cost of the federal employee retirement and fringe benefits—about $13.5 billion of $17.7 billion for 1975.

It is well known that thousands of federal bureaucrats have not repaid their educational loans and that little or nothing is done to collect them. In Detroit, a couple of years ago, 53 employees of the IRS were found to be receiving various forms of welfare by declaring themselves unemployed indigents.

I have learned that some federal employees do not even come to work at all, but receive their salaries anyway. A great many others do little or nothing. Hordes of others spend their time harassing productive business and citizens.

Collectively, they cost the taxpayers about $100 billion a year, compared to $350 million in the 1920s. There were 339,000 in 1975 with salaries averaging $40,000 a year, an amount which has increased substantially since. The interest on the federal debt plus the cost of the bureaucracy consumes almost all the money collected from the personal federal income tax.

The new Energy Department, with its 20,000 employees, costs $12 billion a year, and, so far as I can see, does nothing but damage; CETA disburses enormous amounts for such projects as the $640,000 it spent to provide educational services for the gay (homosexual) community of Los Angeles alone. Is there no better way to waste the taxpayers' hard-earned money?

At the same time the Postal Service has deteriorated, its prices have increased about 500 percent. Even though it pays no taxes, it must be heavily subsidized because of its wasteful and inefficient operation.

By contrast, I note that 30 years ago, it cost me $12 minimum to make a transcontinental telephone call; now I can dial the same phone for as little as 35 cents. While the post office pays no taxes on its real estate, the telephone company in Arizona is the largest contributor of such taxes in the state. And it pays huge state and federal income taxes, in addition to disbursing many millions of dollars in the form of dividends to investors. The taxpayers are the unrequited investors in the post office.

In 1975, 732,000 retirees from federal service were paid $5.2 billion in cash benefits, or $7,150 a year, or $596 a month—sums which have approximately doubled since then. At the same time, 20,015,000 SS retirees were paid $42.6 billion a year, or $2,130 each—$177 a month.

I asked in a previous article why the federal employees do not or cannot finance their own retirement as do those on Social Security. If they were to do so at the present rate of benefits, they would have to contribute well over 30 percent of their incomes for this purpose. On the other hand, if such payments were placed into individual interest-bearing accounts, like Keogh trusts, they could draw approximately their present benefits without increasing their contributions or compelling the taxpayers to underwrite 80 percent of the cost.

But who would ever expect the federal government to do anything as sensible as that? Anyone who does so must indeed have been "born yesterday."

# Foreign Investment Immunity

When, some time ago, I wrote that multi-nationals doing business in the U.S. are exempt under Sec. 892 of the IR Code from taxation on capital gains in this country, there was a storm of protests and denials.

However, the Revenue Act of 1978 establishes beyond question that not only such corporations but even individuals are immune to such levies. It declares: "Nonresident aliens and foreign corporations . . . are exempt from capital gains tax on the sale of capital assets generally, and nonbusiness real estate in particular . . . Foreign investors can generally avoid most or all U.S. taxes on U.S. real estate, including both taxes on current income and gain on sale, by utilizing U.S. tax treaties."

Since such treaties, which exist with 30 countries, are reciprocal, the same advantages of course are accorded American citizens with business interests in these countries.

We know, therefore, that no capital gains tax is due from an American citizen to the country in which he has a capital gain.

I know, furthermore, that many Americans have incorporated their domestic businesses in the Cayman Islands and pay no capital gains taxes on transactions actually completed within the U.S.

Part III of Schedule B of the 1978 income tax return is called "Foreign Accounts and Foreign Trusts." Under Sec. A, the taxpayer is asked whether he has an interest in, or authority over, a financial account in any foreign country. Section B asks whether he was the grantor of, or transferee to, a foreign trust. "If the answer is 'Yes,' you may be required to file forms 3520, 3520-A, or 926."

There is, however, no demand for information in regard to capital gains. Everyone is "required" to answer "Yes" or "No"; but nothing happens when no response is given.

The 1978 "Instructions for Form 1040," page 18, state that if a taxpayer's income in the form of interest from a foreign account exceeds $1,000, he is to get Form 90-22 to discover whether he is considered to have an interest in, or authority over, a bank, security or other financial account in a foreign country. However, this is not sent to the IRS; it is not a tax return; it should simply be forwarded to the Department of the Treasury.

So far as we have been able to discover, there have never been any repercussions for failure to file this form.

It is true that Sec. 904 (b) (3) (E) imposes taxation upon certain capital gains accruing to American citizens from foreign transactions. However, we know of no method by which the IRS can obtain pertinent information in regard to an ordinary individual; nor does the income tax form demand any specific data concerning it.

One additional observation: I have known several Americans who invested heavily in Mexican securities; and, since the government there did not release any information in regard to these, no income therefore was ever reported to the IRS by the investors, nor was any tax ever paid.

Consider, for a moment, the devastating possibilities of Sec. 892 and the existing reciprocal treaty laws. The OPEC countries, which now receive more than $40 billion a year for oil, can buy unlimited amounts of real estate in the U.S. and pay no taxes on any capital gains which may result from such investments; and, in most cases, none on current income either.

# Ch. 5

# Welfare, Waste, and Washington

# Socialism Exposed

I recall vividly the siren songs of the socialists back in the 1930s. In order to create jobs and prosperity for all—so they said—it would only be necessary to reduce the profits of the greedy and parasitical capitalists. Now that some form of at least quasi-socialism has been established in most of the countries of the Western World, we know:

● What these propagandists really wanted; and

● What results may be considered inevitable as they gain more and more power.

The first objective of all such regimes is the impoverishment and destruction of all middle-class business. Centralized governments, controlled by bureaucracies, hate the independent entrepreneur—because he cannot be controlled, his income cannot be accurately determined and, most of all, he tends to think for himself in the political sphere, and therefore presents an implacable opposition to Big-Brother government.

The middle class is, therefore, the only bastion for the continuance of any republican, representative or responsible government.

The second prime objective of all socialist-communist-bureaucratic regimes is to take over as much as possible of the nation's business after the independents have been liquidated. This is an inevitable consequence. The consequent waste and inefficiency in government operation are simply staggering.

Their third great objective is to establish themselves as a ruling elite. The greater their power, the more complete will this process become. In the U.S., the federal bureaucracy is now costing the taxpayers well in excess of $100 billion a year for maintenance and perquisites. In Sweden, the proportional ratio is even greater; in countries like the Soviet empire and Red China, the communist masters have simply taken the places of the old aristocrats and warlords. Every vestige of economic independence has been extirpated. The producers are little more than slaves.

In the earlier stages of the socialist-communist development, these potential future rulers are compelled to observe certain laws; i.e., they cannot immediately confiscate the property of opponents. They therefore establish welfare states, under which they tax the producers, especially the middle class, as nearly as possible to the point of starvation, so that they can live very well indeed and bribe a great number of nonproducers to vote them into office and perpetuate them there.

Once the middle class has been eliminated, the transition to a completely authoritarian police state is comparatively easy, and there is no further need for bribery to purchase votes. The iron fist then emerges from behind the welfare facade in full force, and dissidents are simply shot or sent into exile.

**SECRET WAR**

At the present time, in the U.S. and in such European countries as Britain, Sweden, Norway, Denmark, West Germany, France and Italy, war is in full progress between the bureaucracy, on the one hand, and the producers, especially the middle class, on the other. The latter are fighting everywhere, tooth and nail, to prevent their own total extinction as self-reliant individuals.

I have written a great deal about the situation in the U.S. Reliable authorities estimate that the middle class is now retaining about $500 billion of unreported and untaxed income.

According to an Associated Press article published July 11, a similar battle is raging in Western Europe. Tax cheaters and moonlighters, we read, are costing hard-pressed governments there an estimated $60-billion loss in revenue annually.

**UNDERGROUND ECONOMY**

Actually, no one knows, or can know, the extent of this tax evasion. The taxing agencies are now, as in years past, attempting to crack down on the evaders. The so-called "black economy" dwarfs all other problems existing in England, declares its treasury minister.

In Italy, the communist mayor of Naples abandoned his campaign to "clean up" the tax mess in the city when he discovered how many people would become unemployed as a result of success in such an endeavor. The city exports 5 million pairs of gloves a year, but has not a single legal glove factory.

The money saved by tax evasion accrues not only to the rich, but to lawyers, doctors, farmers and a host of others battling ruinous inflation and confiscatory taxation. Thus, tax resistance has been developed into a fine art.

It is estimated that one-third of all wages in Western Europe remain unreported for tax purposes. In France, the resulting losses are estimated at more than 100 billion francs ($16 billion)—equal to the annual deficit.

In Italy, an estimated one-third of the gross national product (GNP) remains untaxed. In Sweden, the black economy has increased 10-fold during the last 15 years. One-third of the jobs in Stockholm are said to exist in the underground.

In Britain, it is estimated that:

● 15 percent of the GNP goes untaxed;

● At least one taxpayer in five is "on the fiddle"; and

● The true percentage may be no less than 40.

This is primarily a war between socialist bureaucracies and the middle class. The outcome will determine the course and destiny of civilization, perhaps for centuries to come. Unless the bureaucrats are defeated, the entire Western World will probably be plunged into a universal communist hell. It is as simple as that.

# Socialist Inefficiency

After a brief but strong attraction to the mirage of Socialism during the depths of the Great Depression, I had what I call my illumination in 1935 when I arrived at an irreversible conclusion that individual freedom (the most precious thing on this earth) is totally incompatible with any form of totalitarian government, whether it be called communist, socialist, or simply a bureaucratic welfare state. After two years spent in lethargy, I went to work in 1935 with great vigor, established my own independent business, and embarked on the career that has kept me going at high speed for more than 45 years.

The conclusion at which I arrived then is constantly being fortified and reinforced by additional evidence. There is no substitute for private initiative. Had my business establishment been operated by bureaucrats, I have no doubt that it could have been done only with subsidies of at least $50,000 a year.

Interestingly enough, under a heading called THE SPOTLIGHT, the Arizona "Republic" on December 11, 1977, published a review of a book by Ephraim Sevela entitled "Farewell Israel!" in which the author (who had arrived as an emigrant from Russia filled with starry hopes and dreams) describes the operation of its socialist economy. During its 29 years in power, states the author, the labor government managed to combine the worst features of socialism and capitalism: the bureaucrats were omnipresent, lazy, arrogant, incompetent, corrupt, and destructive. Israel survived as a nation of mendicants, who begged for subsistence from the U.S. and world Jewry. The descendants of the Khazar converts to Judaism who arrived from Europe looked with contempt upon the Semitic Jews who arrived from Arab countries and who now constitute a majority in the population.

Wherever socialist enterprise had been established, he found a state of shambles and collapse. Two factories, one privately owned, the other state-operated, produced the same goods; the former produced better merchandise; was able to show a reasonable profit; sold its product at lower prices; and paid exorbitant taxes. The other produced inferior goods and operated at a heavy deficit; of course, it paid **NO** taxes. The author discovered that workers in the state-controlled plant performed only two hours of desultory work during a daily shift.

After all, why should it be otherwise? When all receive the same pay whether they produce or not, why should anyone labor with diligence? But what happens when, one day, there is no one to produce? The inevitable result must be beggary or starvation, which aptly describes the state of Israel.

The reason private business has been forced to raise prices results from federally caused inflation and taxes upon business. However, the post office, which pays no taxes but receives heavy subsidies, has raised its rates 800 percent and its service has deteriorated. Meanwhile the telephone companies, which pay heavy real estate and income taxes, have reduced their rates and improved their service almost beyond comparison. This is free enterprise in operation.

# The Welfare Empire

"An Inventory of Federal Transfer Programs," by William Lawrence and Stephen Leeds (Institute for Socioeconomic Studies, White Plains, N.Y.), lists 182 programs and agencies under which nearly $250 billion was disbursed in 1977.

The first fact which smites the reader is that a great many of these programs are redundant, overlap and are so constituted that no one can discover how much goes for a single general purpose, how many government employees are involved, or what could be done to consolidate the activities or establish some degree of efficiency therein. The amount of money spent, which must be collected from the taxpayers or expended as inflation-creating deficits, is simply mind-boggling: it is beyond human comprehension.

This $250 billion does not include:

• Grants or fellowships for advanced study or research, or for any program not intended primarily to relieve low-level poverty;

• Grants or subsidies to business or to individuals in their roles as producers, investors, or factory owners in the marketplace;

• Funding for public services, facilities, or projects accessible to the general public or for the benefit of communities as a whole; and

• Protective or custodial services for wards of the state, such as homeless children, juvenile offenders, prisoners, or mental incompetents.

These additional programs encompass tens of billions of dollars.

Nor does this volume cover any of the welfare expenditures of state, county, or municipal governments, which constitute untold additional billions.

Glancing through the summaries offered of the 182 federal welfare-transfer programs, we find such items as the following (in billions):

Medicaid, $9.859; Aid to Dependent Children, $5.718; Federal Civil Service Pensions, $6.370; Military Nondisability Retirement, $7.233; Food Stamps, $5.474.

These are mere samples. I know a perfectly healthy and robust man in his 40's who said he became "nervous" as a schoolteacher, quit work and has now for some years been drawing several hundred dollars a month from the federal government because of his "disability."

Although the computations do not include $24.461 billion disbursed by the federal government for "Research and Development" or $15.485 billion given as grants to elementary, secondary, and higher educational institutions, one small item of $1,461 billion attracted my attention. It is called Basic Educational Opportunity Grants, and consists of outright gifts to students on the basis of "need."

Benefits, we read, "not exceeding one-half of their needs" are given to students "in the form of cash, funded through the institutions acting as disbursing agents. About two million students receive grants averaging $900 yearly." Thus more than 20 per cent of all college and post-secondary students receive up to one-half of their "needs" in this one program alone.

This is only one element in the welfare state which keeps some 10 million of our youth technically from being unemployed; and does so at an overall cost of something like $50 billion a year.

# The Welfare Ripoff

I never cease marvelling, first, at the fervor with which the IRS agents seek to collect money not due from small proprietors.

For example, literally thousands of federal bureaucrats obtained their education from government loans, and despite earning large salaries from the same government, do not and are not required to pay what they owe—although nothing should be easier than to collect on such debts.

Health and Human Services admits being ripped off by frauds of at least $9 billion a year; so far officials have been unable to reduce such losses. Some time ago 53 IRS employees in Detroit were caught obtaining government payments—as if they had been jobless and destitute.

The Social Security Administration now pays out about $12 billion a year for disability; but some recipients turned out to be basketball stars earning $30,000 to $40,000 a year.

I know a woman who has been lying on her back for the last eight years and who has cost the taxpayers perhaps a hundred thousand dollars for medical care which has accomplished precisely nothing for this hypochondriac. I know a big, husky fellow who spends his time watching TV and lives very well on disability because teaching made him "nervous."

When I left Detroit in 1960, already 65,000 illegitimate children were on Aid to Dependent Children (ADC), costing the taxpayers $90 million a year, 43 percent of which went to the bureaucrats who administered the program. And then there were the two professors who received a grant of $95,000 to observe, and report on, the operation of bordellos in a South American country.

There is not the slightest doubt that at the present time it is costing the taxpayers at least $100 billion a year to pay out money to people who are utterly undeserving and who are not in need—and to pay the bureaucrats who are disbursing this money.

Occasionally, an especially interesting tidbit gets into the news. According to the Arizona "Republic" of June 14, 1978, one woman in Los Angeles collected $240,000 in welfare for the support of 47 non-existent children. Why not? Surely, no federal bureaucrat would be so impolite as to investigate the claims of a "client" making an application for subsidies as if such client could possibly be guilty of fraud.

In addition to the $240,000, this woman also received food stamps and other types of welfare. Unfortunately for her, the various fraudulent activities in which her common-law husband was engaged eventually led to her own exposure. Otherwise, she might have increased her mythical progeny to 100—and her welfare emoluments in proportion. Incidentally, in addition to many other luxuries, she owned and drove a Porsche, a Cadillac and a Mustang.

This reminds me of the woman who lived in an apartment which I owned in Detroit and who had married 18 service men during World War II. She collected allotments from all of them. Finally, however, when the mailman became intrigued and suspicious because of the 18 checks made out in different names but all delivered to the same box, he reported this to the Department of Defense. As a result, the government punished her by cutting off the allotments. Nothing more.

# *Waste and Deficits*

The government *could* reduce expenditures to a point where, even at its present level of unconstitutional activity, it could eliminate:

● The personal income tax, which yielded $153.1 billion; and

● The corporate, which produced $56.6 billion in 1977.

Together these two taxes produced revenues of $209.7 billion, out of a total income to the government of $354 billion and expenditures of $411.2 billion, with a resulting deficit of $57.2 billion ("1977 Statistical Abstract" p. 249).

At the present time, 2.5 million overpaid and underworked federal employees (outside the Post Office system) cost the taxpayers at least $65 billion a year, in addition to a retirement plan which consumes about $17 billion, of which the bureaucrats contribute less than $3 billion. If federal employees were to finance their own retirement, as everyone on Social Security does, taxes could be reduced by $13 billion for this item alone.

In 1963, the Higher Facilities Education Act was passed, and, in 1965, the Elementary and Secondary Education Act. Since then, allocations under these programs (the real purpose of which is to control ideology in all educational institutions) has risen to more than $16 billion. Since they did very well without any federal subsidy before 1964, they could easily have continued on the same basis; and could return to it at any time.

A few years ago, the government dreamed up a system by which it hoped to control all other levels of political administration. This was called revenue sharing. Some $10 billion is now dished out annually under this program, which has certainly not reduced local taxation anywhere.

Various agencies make grants for a multitude of so-called research projects. Typical among these were $65,000 provided for a man who wrote an essay on why children fall off tricycles; $97,000 for two professors so that they might observe the operation of bordellos in Peru and large amounts to study the mating habits of cockroaches.

It is estimated the government allocates some $80 billion for research. None has the slightest constitutional authority, and very little has any value. Obviously, grants for such purposes are made only to give bureaucrats something to occupy their time, and to ensure the loyalty to the Establishment of the hundreds of thousands of parasites who receive the grants.

Remember, it is precisely this deficit spending which causes our deadly, all-engulfing inflation.

To illustrate the nature of this disease, consider colleges, some of which receive many millions of dollars from the government—often in excess of one-fourth of their entire budgets. But the tragedy is that as a result of such profligacy, the institutional expenditure per student in higher education has risen from $800 in 1955 to $4,000 in 1979-80. And thus, while the subsidies have incresed, their own expenditures, financed from other sources, have risen by 300 percent.

The federal government could reduce its expenditures by $100 billion simply by terminating its own taxes; and it could more than eliminate its present deficit spending merely by eliminating the four kinds of unconstitutional expenditures pinpointed in this article.

But we must understand that the great army of federal bureaucrats will fight tooth and nail to retain all these programs, not because they wish to help others or have any interest in education or welfare, but because much of the money used to fund such programs goes simply for the support of the people who administer them.

# Waste Eats up Billions

According to a recent release from the Associated Press, Deputy Attorney General Benjamin Civiletti declared in official testimony before the Senate Budget Committee that an estimated 10 percent of the entire federal budget is either wasted or stolen outright. There are so many departments, agencies and overlapping programs and such a complexity in their administration that it is utterly impossible to monitor this waste and theft. However, we can be certain that this is no accident: for the whole federal government has become, by design, a vast system of confusion, unnecessary expenditure, and uneconomic proliferation that defies analysis.

Since even some of the prestigious bureaucrats themselves now admit that 10 percent of the budget is lost through waste or theft, we must conclude that disbursements could be reduced for fiscal 1980 by $53 billion without taking a single penny from any activity which has the slightest rationale or justification for its existence. Illegitimates could still be supported; 10 percent of the population could still enjoy food stamps; millions of students could continue to receive taxpayer subsidies; 80 percent of the federal employee retirement cost could still be funded by the taxpayers; and a thousand other unconstitutional programs could still flourish. All that would be necessary to balance the budget would be a partial elimination of current waste and theft.

The Department of Health, Education and Welfare (HEW), which admitted that it disbursed $8 or $9 billion in fraudulent claims in 1977, plans to increase its expenditures from $135 billion to $205.1 billion in 1980. For example, members of a communal cult living in an apartment building were all drawing disability from HEW because they had been certified as "schizophrenic" by one psychiatrist.

The press has occasionally featured articles describing the embezzlements which have become a way of life in the General Services Administration (GSA). We believe that 20 percent of its $5-billion budget has been stolen by federal personnel and suppliers and contractors who are paid for goods never delivered and for work never performed. After receiving their payments, these contractors share their loot with GSA bureaucrats.

Millions of students receive guaranteed loans in addition to grants. According to an article in the Arizona "Republic" on March 6, the default rate on such loans "tops 50 percent at 200 colleges"; the losses to the taxpayers over a period of years run into the billions.

But why should the bureaucrats care? It is not *their* money. And they get almost as much for administering the programs as the totals on which default ensues. Any private businessman, operating in a similar manner, would either become bankrupt, or a prison inmate.

But the far-off federal government is different—it takes the bread out of the mouths of productive citizens and enriches millions of parasites, among whom the principal beneficiaries are the bureaucrats themselves, who administer this multitude of complex and incomprehensible federal programs at a cost of untold billions of dollars.

# *Grants and Disabilities*

The Department of Health and Human Services (HHS) is now by far the largest operation conducted by the federal government. In 1977, HHS disbursed $135 billion a sum which increased to a projected $199,427,676,000 for fiscal 1980, even though it has officially admitted it paid at least $6 to $8 billion in completely fraudulent claims.

It spends at least $2 billion in outright grants to two million college and university students whose parents are below the decent middle-income level; it also makes other funds available to "disadvantaged" and "minority" students; but it will not underwrite even a loan for capable and ambitious young men and women whose parents make enough money to pay heavy income and Social Security taxes, but who cannot afford to pay $6,000 or more annually in non-deductible expenditures to maintain their children at institutions of higher learning.

These are therefore overloaded with students who have little or no ambition or incentive to learn, while those who could profit are denied admission. Incidentally, this practice is very similar to that in communist countries, where the offspring of the hated bourgeoisie are sent to slave-camps, while the proletarians consume the educational budget, no matter how inept they may be intellectually.

The "Aid to Dependent Children" program, under which the government now disburses some $12 billion or more a year, is used almost exclusively to support some 11 or 12 million illegitimate black and chicano children who have "no father in the house." Many of these live in far greater, tax-free affluence than do the self-reliant, taxpaying citizens who pay the bills and who hardly have enough left to feed and clothe their own children in decency.

Even worse is the fact that these hordes of parasites are growing up to spawn large broods of their own who will one day live in the same manner and vote for the politicians who provide such a way of life for them.

Although we certainly do not think that veterans should be short-changed, we cannot understand why $3.683 billion should be expended for their educational assistance many years after the last one was discharged from service. This sum would be sufficient to maintain every soldier who spent any time in Vietnam with an annual scholarship of at least $6,000.

Furthermore, we cannot understand why $1.87 billion should be allocated for non-service-connected disabilities. There is no justification for the above expenditure of $5.553 billion. Many other programs are equally without merit or necessity. We might note that our adventure in Vietnam, totally without useful result, will ultimately cost the American taxpayers $1 trillion.

None of the HHS disbursements has any constitutional authority. Those which serve any justifiable purpose could and should be implemented and administered by the state or local authorities at less than half of the cost expended by the federal government.

Even if HHS were to continue all programs that serve any valid purpose, its expenditures could certainly be reduced by at least $30 billion.

# The Curse of Inflation

On April 29, 1979, the Associated Press released an article giving statistics on the cost of maintaining a family of four on low, middle and higher levels in different parts of the country. The middle-level income (allowing nothing for savings or the creation of a small estate) ranged from $16,211 in Austin, Texas, to $23,099 in Honolulu. The average was about $19,000. In 1915, a family of four could live very well on an income of $2,500 or less.

And this brings us to a consideration of the nature, the causes and the results of inflation, for which the federal government is totally responsible. If it is not reversed in the near future, it will destroy the intangible accumulations of the middle class, and, we can be sure, the very basis of our society.

Debasement of its currency, more than any other factor, brought on the destruction of the Roman Empire and the onset of the Dark Ages, which continued for a thousand years.

It was the fiat currency issued by the government of France after the revolution of 1789 which brought Napoleon to power. After the paper money (the "assignats" and the "montats") served as material for bonfires in the streets of Paris, the Corsican adventurer took over; and he paid in gold on the barrelhead as he marched his armies across Europe for 16 years. We know, therefore, that there was no shortage of specie, any more than there is now in the U.S.

The 1921-23 inflation in Germany finally caused the price of bread to reach 1 trillion marks for a loaf at the same time as a $20 gold piece was sufficient to buy an apartment building or a shopping center. It was this development which wiped out the middle class and created the basis for National Socialism.

History is replete with similar examples. There has never been a single instance in which fiat currency has failed to bring inflation, political turmoil, and eventual revolution or social collapse . . . or perhaps a dictatorship, military or otherwise.

It was their experience with fiat currency during the War of the Revolution—when the paper Continental dollar finally became totally worthless—that prompted our Founding Fathers to establish a solid means of exchange based on specie and to declare that no state shall make anything but gold and silver coin a tender in the payment of debts.

After the terrible inflation which occurred in Sweden following the military adventures of King Charles XII, that country was saved from collapse and destruction by adopting the monetary reforms advanced by Emanuel Swedenborg, which restored the nation to a solid, specie-backed currency.

Let me give some instances from personal experience which illustrate the nature of inflation. In 1951, I made a tour of Italy. In Rome, our group had a 69-year-old guide who had worked, sacrificed and saved for 40 years so that he might retire to live in comfort on the income from his investments. But then the lira was devalued from 5 to an American dollar to 780, and his life's savings were barely sufficient to maintain him for three months.

In 1924, I built a house in Ypsilanti, Mich., at a total cost of $5,400. In 1977, it·was sold for $55,000. The carpenter who received $1.25 an hour in 1924 was better off than his counterpart who was paid $12.50 in 1979-80.

In 1928, working for an insurance company, I found $600 in my pay envelope one Saturday—no deductions whatever. In 1979-80, in order to have similar buying power, I would need at least $6,000; actually, my pay would have to be $12,000, because one-half would go for Social Security, for state and federal income taxes, and other deductions.

At the present rate of inflation, it will take $1,000 in 1989 to buy what $100 now commands. In other words, the car that now costs $6,000 ($600 in 1928-29) will be priced at $60,000. And the $10,000 savings account or insurance policy will buy only a couple of suits, plus perhaps a pair of shoes. In other words, almost all American retirees will be in the position of my Italian guide. Gold may go to $1,000 an ounce.

It should be obvious to any teenager and even to the more intelligent members of Congress that if the present trends continue, we face one of the following crisis situations:

1. A massive tax-revolt;
2. Total economic collapse;
3. Violent revolution; or
4. A mandatory and basic reconstruction of our federal government.

Let us hope that in this country we will have the wisdom and the courage to avoid the tragedies that have overtaken all the great previous cultures of history.

Since the steps that must be taken to save our nation are so obvious, we believe it possible that our electorate may comprehend them in time to send men to Congress who will do what is necessary to restore constitutional government without a bloodbath or the utter collapse of our economy. These are:

• A balanced federal budget and a good start at reducing the federal debt;
• A solid currency based on specie;
• The repeal of the Federal Reserve Act and its replacement with a constitutional monetary system;
• The replacement of the Social Security system with a Universal Trust Plan; and
• Limiting Congress to the activities mandated in Art. I, Sec. 8, of the Constitution.

By effecting such a reconstruction, our nation, the greatest on earth, will have a future more glorious than its past instead of undergoing the doom which will otherwise become inevitable.

# Deadly Forces

Thomas Jefferson warned the American people they must secure their rights with the chains of Constitution while the lessons of the Revolutionary War were still vivid in their memories; for the time would come before very long when they would be so busy making a living and earning money that they would have no time or energy to bring government mismanagers to justice.

No truer statement was ever made. As the productivity of Americans increased dramatically and offered much increased living standards for the future, the politicians gradually discovered that it was easier and politically safer to rob the producers than it was to deny the desires and the demands of parasites.

Thus the way to perpetuate themselves in office was to take from the creators of wealth the fruits of their labor and disburse this among themselves and give it to leeches.

**SYSTEM OF PLUNDER**

This was the basic incentive that spawned the welfare state, which has now become a vast system of legalized but un-Constitutional robbery. How long could the present federal government go on as it now functions, were it not for the votes of those who live, without production, by robbing others?

In 1978, there were 180 federal agencies which disbursed $249 billion in so-called "transfer payments"—a sum which has now increased to at least $350 billion. This does not include the cost of the bureaucracy, the interest on the federal debt and various other expenditures, such as payments to elementary, secondary and higher education.

This is also the reason for deficit spending, which has caused the inflation that is now ruining the American people, and that, in turn, has made it necessary to increase Social Security (SS) and other pension payments until retirees have become virtual wards of the state and an intolerable burden upon the producing class.

This creeping cancer can result only in the destruction, not only of the American republic, but of the foundation for our culture. Millions of women—especially Blacks and Chicanos—are encouraged to breed flocks of illegitimate children who live on government (taxpayer) handouts and who will one day rear millions of children who can only repeat what their parents have done. As they grow, they become avid supporters of the welfare state; and our population is transformed more and more into such entities.

But they constitute only one segment of this fearful problem. Self-respecting and self-supporting families can scarcely afford children, because they must pay such enormous taxes to support the illegitimates and other welfare recipients.

The "Social Insecurity" program is another example of what is driving our nation into despair and bankruptcy. Whereas now, only 2 percent of Americans reaching the age of 65 are said to be financially independent, 85 or 90 percent could be so under a "universal trust plan" (SPOTLIGHT, Feb. 28, 1983), which would cost the younger generations nothing and would provide ample retirement funds for almost the entire population at far less cost than must now be spent for SS. But this is not permitted because it would interfere with the system of fractional reserve banking, under which the bankers collect hundreds of billions of interest annually without actually lending any money at all.

Thus, in America today, we have a vast system of legalized robbery—for that is what it is. And now, since theft has become almost universal, more and more people are becoming dishonest. One half of the population studies methods by which to steal more, and the other half develops its resources to protect what possessions they have.

The very rich protect themselves by means of loopholes and other devices in the Internal Revenue Code, planted there for their benefit. The welfare recipients organize and bring pressure on the politicians to obtain more of it. They have plenty of time to do this, for they are making a career of this activity.

**TAX REBELLION**

On the other hand, the middle-class producers are trying to protect what they have from being ravaged by the government. Since they have not had much success in reforming the Internal Revenue Code for their benefit, they are now engaged in a vast tax rebellion, which involves millions of individuals and which is estimated to have deprived the federal government of somewhere between $100 billion and $150 billion in 1983.

As a result, to meet the resistance of the taxpayers, the Reagan administration has reduced personal income taxes by about 25 percent. But to meet the demands of the SS recipients, the tax for this purpose has risen into the stratosphere.

Thus we have enormous federal budgets coupled with staggering deficits. The admitted federal debt has now risen to about $1.4 trillion—which, plus other federal obligations, amounts to a total of about three times that sum.

In 1983, the budget was $810 billion, of which only about one-fourth was for "defense." In 1984, it will be about $900 billion. And it must increase at this rate or faster unless drastic reforms are instituted very soon.

How long will it be before the United States will go the way of the Roman empire? It is obvious to the objective observer that forces similar to those that detroyed that political entity are doing their deadly work in the land of the free and the home of the brave.

**THOMAS JEFFERSON**
. . . Timely warning.

# Off-Budget Financing

The Federal Financing Bank Act, passed without publicity in December, 1973, created a powerful entity which is part of the U.S. treasury itself and which began operations in May, 1974.

Although only seven individuals conduct its business, it has processed thousands of loans and had accumulated debts exceeding $106 billion by the end of 1981 and had, therefore, become the second largest lending institution in the U.S., surpassed only, and very slightly, by the Bank of America.

Its purpose is to finance undertakings sponsored by a great variety of federal agencies, which were previously underwritten by the issuance of their own securities in the open market.

Some of them still do so, but the majority of all federal loans since 1974 have been through the Federal Financing Bank, which simply accepts the certificates of indebtedness from these agencies and sells them to the treasury, which obtains the necessary funds by issuing its own securities, and thus increases the national debt.

Total outstanding loans in this general category have been growing at an alarming rate. In 1974, the total was $35.4 billion, of which $602 million was financed through the bank. By 1976, the amounts were $85.6 and $48 billion respectively; and in August, 1980, the totals were $127 and $80 billion. As already noted, by December, 1981, the latter amount had increased to nearly $110 billion.

Various federal agencies also lend money, make outright grants, or guarantee loans made by private lenders, among which are billions advanced to college and university students for educational purposes; and tens of billions given for supposed research.

Very little of this money ever returns to the treasury, and it constitutes a constant drain upon the American taxpayers. Among the federal agencies which make loans for specific activities, the following are very important:

● Agency for International Development;

- U.S. Information Agency;
- Federal Home Loan Bank Board;
- Commodity Credit Corp.;
- Rural Electrification Administration;
- Farmers Home Administration schemes;
- U.S. Export-Import Bank;
- Housing and Urban Development Administration;
- Government Mortgage Association;
- Helium Fund;
- Rural Telephone Bank;
- Tennessee Valley Authority;
- Veterans Administration; and
- St. Lawrence Seaway Development Corp.

Among many other expenditures, the government lends money to an agency which finances the export of American-made products to foreign countries. The manufacturers get their money at once; if the foreigners do not pay, the American taxpayers foot the bill. For that is the way the federal government operates.

The ironic element in all this is the fact that the debts of the Federal Financing Bank and other government agencies are treated as "off budget" expenditures. The theory is that since those who receive the money agree to repay it with interest, no actual debt is incurred and that, therefore, no expenditure has taken place.

Nothing, however, could be further from the truth; the money is paid out and the debts outstanding have been, and are, increasing by leaps and bounds to a frightening extent.

In July, 1980, the stated federal debt was $894,454 million; however, federal agencies had on that date paid out $126,762 million more in the form of loans or other advances than they had been repaid. The actual debt, therefore, was not the first figure shown above, but $1,021,216 million. It must now be approaching $1.25 trillion.

Thus the official deficit for fiscal 1981 was $55 billion; but, since the Federal Financing Bank and other agencies increased their loans by at least $20 billion during that period, the actual deficit was not less than $75 billion. And we can be sure that the excess loans contributed exactly as much, dollar for dollar, to inflation, as did the deficits admitted in the regular budget.

These federal operations are highly secret, complex and esoteric. They contribute not only to inflation, but also to high interest rates, and ever-increasing taxation. Furthermore, all this is an additional means by which the central government grows bigger, increasingly oppressive, more powerful and dictatorial, as well as all-encompassing in its activities and control over every facet of private life.

This is neither a full nor comprehensive explanation of the operations of the Federal Financing Bank. Those who wish to study it further can obtain a copy of PL 93-224 from their congressmen or the Document Room, House of Representatives, Washington, D.C. 20515; (202) 225-3456. The "Wall Street Journal" published an excellent article on the subject (Dec. 1, 1981); and the "International Currency Review" included a good analysis of the same (Vol. 12, No. 5, 1980).

Occasionally, some reference to all this appears in the regular press; but, by and large, the public has been kept in the dark concerning it. Very few members of Congress understand, or are aware of, its manifold techniques for plunging this nation into everlasting and inescapable debt, which will inevitably destroy our economy completely, unless drastic measures are taken soon to reverse the trends which have developed during recent years.

# Bloated Bureaucracy

Our huge and bloated federal bureaucracy, generally overpaid and underworked, is beginning more and more to resemble its counterparts in socialist or even in communist countries.

As they assume greater power, they intrude more and more persistently into the lives of our citizens, become more arrogant, consume more of the taxpayers' tributes and edge closer and closer to the totalitarian concepts of life and government.

Operating in tandem with the national and international financiers, they become progressively more burdensome upon the productive members of society. The interest on the federal debt plus the mere cost of maintaining the federal colossus is approaching $300 billion a year—a sum which continues to increase at a horrendous pace.   .

### BUREAUCRATS UNWORRIED

At the present time, this bureaucracy is not concerned over inflation, because its members receive large increases in pay as the value of the currency declines; and the hundreds of thousands on federal pensions also receive large increases annually—the bulk of which comes from the pockets of the taxpayers. This situation constitutes a time bomb, which, when it explodes, must cause untold devastation or even the demise of our system of responsible government.

There is not the slightest doubt in my mind that the federal budget could not only be balanced, but a start made at reducing the federal debt without increasing taxes or eliminating any necessary or Constitutional services, simply by eliminating some of the waste, extravagance and unnecessary expenditures which are now routine operations.

However, all the recipients of these benefits are so determined and so militant in their demands that our pliant Congress dares not assert its authority to deny them. It seems to them, at least for the moment, easier to extort the money from the producers and finance the deficits by increasing the public debt than it would be to bite the bullet and do what wisdom and statesmanship would dictate.

### LUXURIATING

Just as an indication of the contempt and arrogance with which our federal establishment regards the people at large, I will cite information contained in an article written by David Lambro and published on May 9. He states that about 100 expensively outfitted dining rooms are hidden away in various federal departments in Washington, where top bureaucrats dine in style on expensively prepared food at prices lower than the general public pays in hash joints.

These meals, prepared by expert chefs, are comparable to those served in the finest restaurants at prices ranging from $12 to $20; but the bureaucrats pay only from $2 to $4 for them. Last year, the total revenue from these dining rooms was only $500,000; but the actual cost was $2.9 million, of which more than 80 percent was paid by the taxpayers. Now wouldn't you think that public servants who receive from $50,000 to $80,000 in salaries from the taxpayers could afford to pay for their own food?

Of course, this is only a drop in the budget of more than $900 billion. But multiply this a thousand times and you get some idea of how the federal government luxuriates at the expense of the people.   ●

# Ch. 6

# Social (In)Security

# The Social Security Number Bluff

That the IRS, and to a lesser extent other federal agencies, operate on the basis of pure bluff is a fact that every American citizen should understand thoroughly and act accordingly.

One of the most vicious of such bluffs deals with the use of the Social Security number. I remember my religious father telling me when I was a boy that the time would come when everyone would be compelled—in order to buy or sell—to take the Mark of the Beast mentioned in Revelation 13:16-18; 14: 9, 11; 15:2; 16:2; 19:20; and 20:4; and I have encountered those who say that the Social Security number is this Mark of the Beast.

Be that as it may, it is certain that the federal government is avid in its attempts to discover and use the number so that it can determine the income of every person from wages, salaries, rents, dividends, interest, royalties, and even capital gains.

However, the disclosure of this number can be compelled only in documents dealing directly with taxes **and** contributions to, or benefits from, the Social Security system itself. There are six variations of Form 1099, on which various types of payments and income are reported by payers to the IRS and to payees. These cover interest, dividends, commercial rentals, payments to trust beneficiaries, etc. Each has a space for the social security number of the recipient.

I have been told by certain individuals that banks and savings and loan associations have refused to handle accounts without the Social Security number. However, I also know various people who are drawing such revenue without ever revealing or conveying such an identification.

All such demands are based on pressure from the IRS; for if this agency does not possess this number, how will it be able to determine which one of a myriad John Smiths was paid the $15.32 of interest from the Podunk Savings and Loan Association of the State of Erehwon?

Actually, the IRS has tens of billions of such reports, not one of which is required by law to carry the SS number. Any citizen who reveals this unnecessarily is the dupe of a despotic government.

There is a short sentence in Section 1449 of the **Master Tax Guide** of 1977 which disposes of this whole debate: "Payers of dividends, interest, and other payments who must report such payments to the IRS may request the recipient (on Form 3435) to furnish his identifying number (Reg. #301.6109 .1)."

The bank, savings and loan association, securities broker, etc., **may request it**; but this request cannot and need not be enforced.

**(NOTE: The law concerning all this has now been changed. For details, see "Crisis Postponed," p. 112.)**

# The Problems Facing Social Security

Letters frequently ask for an explanation of how to escape the federal Social Security system; and there is nothing I would rather do than offer a sure, simple and legal way to accomplish this.

If your income is from a trust, or in the form of interest, dividends, royalties, capital gains, or certain other so-called "passive" income, it is not subject to Social Security "contributions." You could receive $1 million a year in such payments without owing a cent for the maintenance of the Social Security system.

However, if you work for a private employer or if you are self-employed, the law is quite specific. In the former category, you and your employer are required to pay equal amounts into the employee's account. If self-employed, you are required to send in your own "contributions."

However, if you are a minister, a priest or a rabbi, etc., and receive income from services performed in such capacity, you may leave the Social Security system by filing Form 4363 by the end of the second year in which such income is received.

If you belong to a communal order which requires a vow of poverty, you are excused entirely from participation in the federal Social Security program.

If you belong to the Amish church, you may file IRS Form 4029 and be exempted from the Social Security system. The form does not mention the Amish church by name, but so far as I know the IRS has not granted exemptions to any other church, despite the First Amendment ban on establishment of religion.

Of course, federal employees have not been enmeshed in the SS system. If such individuals leave the service, any cash they have "contributed" may be refunded. For those who remain, the U.S. taxpayers pay approximately 80 percent of their annuities and the cost of other welfare given them.

The whole SS system is facing bankruptcy, eventual collapse, or impossible burdens upon the younger generation, of whom only 75 percent have any hope of ever receiving any benefits under it, since 25 percent die before reaching retirement age.

Furthermore, every person reaching the age of 62 in 1987 will lose his entire "investment" unless he has "contributed" to the system for at least nine full years. And beginning in 1991, the requirement will be for 10 years of "contributions" before any benefits would be available. Hence it is quite possible you may pay taxes into the system and receive no benefits at all.

It is high time that definite steps be taken to phase out the SS system in favor of a Universal Trust Plan, which will create an entirely new society. This will establish irrevocable estates for tens of millions of people and will not cost the younger generation one dime for the support of those who retired. Everyone—under such a system—would finance his own retirement and receive at least four or five times as much for his investment as is now returned under Social Security.

**(NOTE: Under a new law, federal employees now hired for the first time will be enrolled in the SS system.)**

# Who Was Required?

Shortly after I wrote an article stating that the Social Security number is mandatory only on documents relevant to the SS tax and that it need not be given to banks, savings and loan associations, security brokers, etc., I received a small avalanche of mail from people who had been informed by their financial institutions that the law requires such identification on all accounts. The authorities cited were Public Law 87-397 and IRS Regulations 103.26, 31, and 42 pursuant to the Bank Secrecy Act of 1970, Statute 1114.

Public Law 87-397, which was passed on October 6, 1961, was called "An Act to amend the IR Code of 1954 to permit the Use of Identifying Numbers." This became Sec. 6109. Notice it only "permitted" their use, but did not require it except when one person prepares a 1040 or a similar report for another.

However, this section was amended as of December 31, 1976, by adding subsec. (a) (4), which explains the duties of tax-preparers as they relate to the inclusion of SS numbers. Then, to clarify the matter further, the subsection states that within the meaning of the law, the word "return" shall include only such documents as are defined in sec. 669 (e)—where we learn that "return" means only a report disclosing the tax-liability of a taxpayer.

The extent to which the IRS seeks to deceive by doubletalk becomes evident after a study of regulations 103.21 through 103.42, which cover "Reports Required to Be Made" (subpart B); "Records Required to be Maintained" (subpart C); and "General Provisions" (subpart D). Remember that these are only bureaucratic regulations, have not been tested in the courts, do not have the force of law and do not carry any sanctions.

As we stated in our previous article, the financial institution may "request" his SS number from any depositor. However, it is not mandatory that this be given, as regulation 103.34 (a) (1) makes clear and which we now quote so that our readers may be better able to use it:

"With respect to each deposit or share account, opened with a bank after June 30, 1972, by a person residing or doing business in the United States or by a citizen of the United States, such bank shall, within 45 days from the date such an account is opened, secure and maintain a record of the taxpayer identification number of the person maintaining the account; . . . In the event that a bank has been unable to secure the identification required herein with respect to an account within the 45-day period specified, it shall nevertheless not be deemed to be in violation of this section if:

"(i) It has made a reasonable effort to secure identification and

"(ii) It maintains a list containing the names, addresses, and account numbers of those persons from whom it has been unable to secure such identification, and makes the names, addresses, and account numbers of these persons available to the Secretary as directed by him."

Nothing could be plainer: the bank may ask for an identification (SS) number within 45 days after the account is opened; but it must continue accounts and pay interest on them even if it cannot obtain such identification number.

Regulation 103.35 (a) (1) contains the same provisions in regard to brokers and dealers in securities.

(However, see p. 112 for revisions in the law.)

# Carter's Social Security Bill

The Social Security system, which started as a purring kitten in 1936, has become a ravenous tiger, growing more gluttonous and destructive every year.

Consider that:

● (1) About one-fourth of all individuals who contribute to the system will not live to receive any returns for their contributions;

● (2) If the same amount of money were placed in an inviolable trust, the benefits would remain under any circumstances and would be at least four times those possible under Social Security; and

● (3) Taxes have to be paid on the contributions which all individuals who work for wages or salaries are forced to make to the program.

Oh, what a triple insult!

What with inflation, the falling birth-rate, greater longevity, and the increasing number of disabled persons, the Social Security System, faced with imminent bankruptcy, forced the government to adopt draconian measures to prevent a revolt by organized retirees, who have become the virtual wards of the state.

To compound the difficulties impending, millions of adults have faked or developed some kind of disability which entitles or at least enables them to draw federal handouts for the remainder of their lives. Such recipients are now costing the taxpayers $10 billion a year (in 1975, there were 4,124,800 of these who received $7,629,400,000).

I know one healthy-looking man in his 40's who is drawing $250 a month, while his wife works; and a woman who has been lying on her back for eight years and who has consumed more than $100,000 of federal largesse in medical care and other payments.

In order to pay for these programs, which give jobs to about 60,000 bureaucrats, the cost of Social Security to a man or woman who earns $42,600 in 1986 (which by then may not be enough to support a decent living standard for a family of five) will be $3,046, with an equal inflation-causing amount taken from his or her employer—a total of $6,092. If this sum were invested for 40 years annually in a personal cumulative trust at 5 per cent, the corpus thereof would total nearly $800,000; and would pay a monthly annuity of $4,000 without reducing the principal. At 6 per cent, it would pay nearly $7,000 a month for 20 years.

Once when I appeared on a radio call-in program and quoted these statistics, the MC remarked that no interest-paying investments could be found for the tens of billions of trust funds which might develop under a Universal Trust Plan. Ah, that is precisely the point: and this is the reason why Congress dares not institute such a system. At present, bankers lend out about $3 trillion of created checkbook money, on which they collect about $350 billion of interest annually. Trust funds, with real assets, would replace this checkbook money, created out of nothing; and the same $350 billion would be owed to tens of millions of productive citizens, who would collect this interest from their trust accounts.

The Social Security swindle continues in order to enable parasitical bankers to collect trillions of dollars from the American producers.

What solution, then, would I suggest? I believe that the federal government should:

● (1) Repay to every present contributor to Social Security whatever sum he has already invested in the system;

● (2) Require that this be placed in an irrevocable trust to mature at age 60 or thereabouts; and

● (3) Make the worker thereafter pay at least 5 percent of his income up to $1,500 a year into this trust until maturity, such payments to be deductible from taxable income.

# Coping with Social Security Tax Problems

There are many ways in which wage-workers or even the salaried are coping with their income-tax problems.

For example, a great many are renting two or three rooms in their homes or one or two apartments or light housekeeping units without disclosing the income therefrom.

Others, such as plumbers, carpenters, electricians, etc., employed by corporations, do considerable moonlighting, which they consider nobody's business but their own.

**However, one of the significant and substantial recent developments consists of "going on contract." Under this procedure, the employer signs a formal contract with his employee to perform certain specific duties for definite sums of money.**

The former employee now becomes an independent entrepreneur and has the status of a self-employed person, as if he were running a business of his own.

He will no longer be eligible for unemployment compensation and certain other potential benefits; but not one cent will be subtracted from his wage or salary for Social Security, state or federal income taxes, union dues, or anything else.

Since, under these circumstances, the employer is released from all the work and expense involved in transmitting payments to government agencies and since he need no longer make any contributions to the state unemployment fund or the Social Security program, he can pay a substantially larger amount for the services rendered.

**The employee, on the other hand, has 100 per cent take-home pay. Of course, as a self-employed person, he is now required to pay his own income taxes directly and make his own total contribution to the SS administration. However, there will be no payments to unemployment funds or other demands.**

Since his own income tax remains the same and since his SS contributions are only slightly more as an entrepreneur than were his own payments as an employee, it is obvious that his economic condition, as well as that of his employer, is much improved by going on contract.

# Social Security vs. Costs and Wages

When an independent contractor, a painter who had one helper, offered to paint my house for $500 I was made painfully aware of the devastating effects of federal income and Social Security taxation upon costs and wages. For when I protested that this price was too high, he explained that, after all, more than one-third of this sum would be snatched from him, as follows:

| | |
|---|---|
| Contract Price | $500.00 |
| For Contractor | 300.00 |
| For Helper | 200.00 |
| For Social Security: | |
| Contractor, at 8% | $24.00 |
| From Helper, at 5.85% | 11.70 |
| Contractor's Contribution | 11.70 |
| Total SS | 47.40 |
| For Income Taxes: | |
| From Helper, at 25% | 50.00 |
| From Contractor, at 30% | 90.00 |
| Total Income Taxes | 140.00 |
| Total for federal government ( 37.48%) | 187.40 |
| Net Remaining for Workers | 312.60 |

However, this is by no means the entire story. For everything these workers must buy costs them at least 30 per cent more because of the income and Social Security taxes built into every item as an integral element in the cost of production. In other words, were it not for these, this contractor and his helper could enjoy the same living standard they now have by performing my job for $210 instead of $500.

Is not this some form of insanity? Is it any wonder that literally millions of jobs such as this remain unreported since people who work hard with their hands would rather risk the dangers of tax-evasion than the certainty of crushing poverty for themselves and for their families? Why should they surrender more than half of their production to a parasitical bureaucracy, which, like the lawyers excoriated by Jesus in the New Testament, never lift their fingers to remove any burden from the backs of the people?

# *Abandoning the Social Security System*

No doubt the inexorable logic of economic compulsion will one day accomplish the demise of our Social Security system; the practical question which will soon be facing the Congress is whether its death will result from statesmanlike foresight or because of a collapse which will bring with it untold suffering and social disruption.

The handwriting on the wall is plain for everyone to observe. When it started in 1936, the maximum contribution was $30 a year; and, for some time, the trust funds continued to increase. All of these, however, were simply appropriated by the federal government in return for IOUs in the form of bonds, and spent for unrelated purposes—a form of theft almost without parallel.

In 1977, the maximum combined employer-employee contribution for each account is $2,032, and the end to this dreadful escalation is not in sight—the reason being in part the ruinous inflation perpetrated by the federal government, coupled with the declining number of contributors and the increasing number of beneficiaries. These latter now approximate one-half the number of the former.

Federal employees were much too clever to be caught in the Social Security hoax and delusion. These people who receive double the pay for half the work required in private employment have an extremely generous retirement plan, to which all American taxpayers contribute annually about $13 billion.

If any federal employee decides to leave the service before retirement benefits become available, all his contributions are returned. Furthermore, he can retire after 20 or 25 years, or even less, and may be able to take another job for many years; and no matter how much he earns, he never suffers any diminution in his federal benefits. Employees who attain a good GS (General Schedule) rating and remain in the federal service 35 or 40 years are eligible to pensions comparable to the emoluments of business executives.

Compare this with the situation of those on Social Security. In the first place, 25 per cent of them die before reaching retirement age, and therefore receive nothing—nor are there any heirs. If one decides to retire at 62 instead of 65, his small benefits are reduced by 20 per cent. Thereafter, he remains under the severest restrictions: for every $2 he earns above a small amount, he will lose $1 of his Social Security.

Since all governmental units have, by their own decision, and by giving two years' notice, been permitted to withdraw from SS—a privilege not extended to such peons as the self-employed or those who work in private endeavor—one city after another has fled the sinking ship.

New York announced in March, 1976, that it would do so, thus depriving the System of $400' million annually. Los Angeles, with 60,000 employees, noting that a program now costing $74 million could be replaced with one costing $22 million and providing the same benefits, is shopping around. Since 1959, 322 local governmental units have abandoned the SS system; many others, one by one, are following suit.

**(NOTE: Employees of state and local governments, as well as of charities, are no longer permitted to withdraw from SS.)**

# Security Solution

I have discussed the impending crisis brought on by the intolerable federal debt and the bankruptcy of the Social Security (SS) system. Now we will consider the only possible solution, a proposal which I have presented to congressional committees and in articles written for The SPOTLIGHT (April 20, 1981).

Interestingly enough, a syndicated article by James Kilpatrick, published on December 4, 1982, gives his full support to a proposal virtually identical to mine, which has been advanced by the National Taxpayers Legal Fund, a Washington-based organization.

The gist of this is that the present system should be phased out during the next 30 or 40 years; that those already retired, and those about to retire, remain in the system; but that all younger workers and the self-employed be excused from SS on condition that they establish their own private retirement funds—similar to the present IRA or Keogh programs. This is precisely what I have been advocating for more than 10 years.

Of course, the practical question arises: How will payments be made to present and future retirees as contributions from workers decline? However, the problem is less economic than political. As private trust funds increase until they total perhaps $35 million and comprise reserves of at least $1 trillion, a reasonable tax can equitably be imposed on the revenues generated during the period of transition.

Furthermore, the federal government could sell its grid complex for perhaps $200 billion, which would then be operated by private enterprise and produce income and property taxes for local governments. It could very well sell a portion of the 765 million acres of land it owns, mostly in the Western states, in violation of the Constitution.

It could stop disbursing some $80 billion a year for silly research grants to favored individuals. As a last resort, it could sell bonds, the interest and repayment of which would be guaranteed by future taxes imposed on the revenues of the millions of growing trust funds. After a few years, when the number of SS retirees has been drastically reduced, such taxation would no longer be necessary.

## BUILD HOUSES

Such trust funds, representing real values, would in 20 years probably total more than $2 trillion. At 8 percent interest, the revenues would be $160 billion, all accruing to the benefit of Americans who worked all their lives to create them. At $3 trillion, the income would be $240 billion, which would eventually go to the millions of retirees. This capital would be used to build housing, shopping centers, office buildings and even for public works.

Of course, the financiers would oppose all this as if it were a death sentence; for, in time, it would put an end to what is known as fractional reserve banking, that greatest of all swindles. Through it, bankers collect hundreds of billions of dollars every year without actually lending any money at all—simply by creating credit on their books.

However, the bankers could still be doing a good business by offering useful services, as they do in Singapore and South Korea, where fractional reserve banking is outlawed—and where, because of this fact and other statesmanlike measures a social and economic miracle has taken place in a few years. Remember that our state governments cannot issue money; and many of them cannot borrow. Yet they give far more in the way of services to the citizens than does the federal colossus.

Consider some of the advantages which would follow the adoption of my proposals. The producers would no longer be forced to support those who have retired; every person would have his own inviolable trust account, which would continue intact whether he lives long enough to retire with an ample pension or leave his money to his children or other heirs and devisees. The government would soon be able to operate without deficits and could undoubtedly make a start at liquidating its debt.

Of course, we assume that deficit spending will be prohibited and that, therefore, inflation will not increase; thus, the value of trust accounts would remain constant.

Now let us glance at what these could and would be. In 1981, the combined employer-employee contribution had risen to 13.4 percent on $29,700, or $3,978 a year—an investment which, at 8 percent cumulative interest, would create a trust fund of $450,000 in 30 years and which would pay a retiree at age 65 $72,000 a year for life; or at least $36,000 without touching the principal.

If a person pays $125 a month into an individual retirement account (IRA) at 8 percent cumulative interest for 40 years, this will total $475,000 and pay $28,500 a year without reducing the corpus.

I have before me a calculation issued by the Western Savings and Loan Association of Arizona which shows that if $2,000 is placed annually into such an account for 40 years at 12 percent interest, an investment of $80,000 will create a fund of $1,534,183, on which monthly interest thereafter can be paid of $15,341.00. At 8 percent, the respective totals would be $1,026,746 and $8,556.00.

We can expect the bureaucrats who administer SS to describe a list of handouts going to non-contributors; but they don't want to discuss the 25 or 30 percent of all contributors who die before retirement or the frightful burdens upon the producers. Nor will they talk about the enormous social advantage of paying interest to millions of savers instead of to the bankers, who collect hundreds of billions by creating credit on their books out of thin air.

Let us note, in closing, that not only Singapore has a system similar to what we are proposing; the same is also true of South Korea, Chile and elsewhere. As more and more Americans become disenchanted with its operation, I believe that something of this kind will become inevitable in the U.S. also. ●

# Crisis Postponed

Do you remember how, in 1977, huge increases in Social Security (SS) taxes were promised as the means of keeping the SS System solvent at least for the remainder of this century—and then how the system went practically bankrupt in 1982?

Now a hodgepodge of provisions—which, for the most part, reduce benefits and increase taxes by $165 billion between 1983 and 1989—is offered as a permanent solution of the system's fiscal problems.

However, even though forcing additional millions into the program may help for a while, it will certainly compound the system's ultimate difficulties. I predict that the solution I have been offering for years will at last become mandatory, simply because no other will meet the final crisis.

Following are the principal provisions of the new SS law:

● In 1990, benefits will be reduced by only $1 for every $3 of income earned by recipients over the ceiling—which is now $6,600—instead of $1 for every $2.

● Starting in 1990, anyone who wishes to continue working but wants to defer benefits will be given increased delayed credits upon retirement. In 2009, this will be an extra 8 percent for each year over 65.

● Beginning in 1983, cost-of-living increases will be given only at the start of the next year.

● Starting in 1985, such increases will be reduced if the fund is near insolvency.

● Beginning in 1984, one-half of the SS benefits will be taxable for individuals with income from any source over $25,000 and, for couples, over $32,000.

● Starting in 1984, rates and amounts subject to taxation will begin earlier than previously scheduled.

● In 1984, the self-employed will begin paying taxes equal to the combined amounts now assessed against employers and employees. Until 1989, there will be a 2.9-percent credit; after that date, the rate of the tax will be reduced, the "losses" to be appropriated from the general budget.

● In 1984, all new federal employees will be forced into the system.

● In 1984, all employees of non-profit institutions and organizations, such as hospitals, will be forced into the system—including lay employees of churches.

● State and other government employees are prohibited from leaving the system.

● In 1983, the Social Security trust funds will receive $18 billion from the general treasury.

● In 1983, the fund will receive $1.1 billion, representing uncashed Social Security checks.

● Beginning with date of enactment, felons serving prison terms will no longer be eligible to receive SS benefits.

● In 1985, benefits will no longer be paid to dependents and survivors of aliens living abroad.

● In 1984, the amounts paid to persons over 60 who have contributed for only a few years will be reduced.

● In the year 2003, the retirement age will be increased in steps until it reaches 66 in 2009; between 2020 and 2027, to 67. Retirees will still be able to draw benefits beginning at age 62, but with actuarily reduced benefits.

● Beginning in 1984, more liberal payments will be paid widows, widowers and divorced persons.

We will see how soon the system will face its next crisis.

# Ch. 7

# Churches, Charity, and IRS Chicanery

# IRS Rules Are Vague

I am often confounded by the misinformation and ignorance concerning the IRS, its laws, regulations and enforcement. Never once in 35 years have I received a useful reply to any question. Either no answer at all came or the information given me was incorrect, misleading or potentially destructive. As a result, I conclude that no one should believe anything an IRS agent may say.

Although CPAs, tax-preparers, counsellors and lawyers stand at a higher cut than IRS personnel, many of them also are guilty of so much error and ignorance that I would never accept anything they say without verification. For example, a number of years ago, after completing a certain business transaction, a tax-lawyer "expert," who was probably earning $100,000 a year, agreed with the IRS that I had incurred a tax liability.

Later, after considerable research, I discovered that both were totally in error; and for years I have been plying the IRS with a demand for an official statement as to whether or not a tax is due in such a deal. Although I have a stack of letters containing doubletalk from high officials, they absolutely refuse to answer my question, which means that no tax was due when it was levied upon me and when the high-priced lawyer agreed.

When I wrote articles stating that no one is required by the law to give his Social Security number to a bank, a savings and loan association, a securities broker or a commercial lessee, I was inundated with letters written to SPOTLIGHT subscribers by tax counsellors and by officials of banks, savings and loan associations, brokers and others, all saying that the law required such identification. They were all wrong; and I have published the regulation which substantiates my original statement.

After I wrote an article stating that no capital-gains tax is due on the sale of depreciable commercial property until the basis has been recovered, I received nearly 50 letters from tax "experts" of various kinds, all of which declared that I was in error. But I was *not* wrong: all of these people, who probably charge between $50 and $100 an hour for giving tax information to their clients, are the ones who are wrong.

And then there was the tragic experience of a longtime Liberty Lobby supporter who engaged a CPA and a lawyer—who charged a substantial fee—for setting up an irrevocable trust with a corpus of $425,000 in such a manner that he had to pay gift taxes of $92,000, after which the IRS attacked him to levy even more. Had the trust been set up properly, not one penny would have been due.

We can only assume that the CPA and the lawyer were merely ignorant, for surely they could not gain anything personally by causing their client an unnecessary loss of about $100,000.

It seems to me that when professionals charge huge prices for services to clients, they should be liable for double damages whenever they cause losses because of ignorance or incompetence.

I have observed lawyers and CPAs for many years; few of them do their homework carefully; many of them are simply contemptuous toward their clients and have no objective except to fleece or betray them. This is not true of all; there are shining and wonderful exceptions. However, it is my suggestion that every person is his own best friend; and before engaging the professional services of another, every person should beware.

# The Universal Life Church

Religious corporations enjoy the highest advantages possible under Secs. 170 and 501 (c) (3) of the IR Code. Their preferential status is automatic—that is, once they are organized, their recognition by IRS is mandatory and not subject to examination and approval as are all others seeking immunity from that agency.

They are not even required to file for exemption with the IRS and they do so only so that contributors may be officially assured that contributions are tax-deductible. What is even more important is the fact that the government has no power to define what constitutes a valid religious belief or entity or who may qualify as a minister in the field of religion.

In 1962, Kirby Hensley, a keen but illiterate individual—who had previously made and lost $1 million twice—organized the Universal Life Church with headquarters in Modesto, California; this has no creed and its only declaration of faith is to do whatever is right.

The IRS, claiming that this corporation could not qualify as a church within the meaning of the IR Code, collected $10,377.20 from Mr. Hensley's church, which thereupon sued for a refund in the U.S. District Court for the Eastern District of California and recovered $11,606.84, including interest, under a decree issued by Judge James F. Battin on March 1, 1974.

The opinion stated that "neither this court, nor any branch of the government, will consider the merits or fallacies of a religion. Nor will the Court compare the beliefs, dogmas, and practices of a newly organized religion with those of an older, more established religion. Nor will the Court praise or condemn a religion, however excellent or fanatical or preposterous it may seem. Were the Court to do so, it would impinge upon the guarantees of the First Amendment.

"In short, the Court merely finds that the plaintiff's ordination of ministers, its granting of church charters, and its issuances of honorary Doctor of Divinity certificates are not substantial activities which do not further any religious purpose."

The far-reaching implications of this decision are that when any three persons organize a church corporation under state law, establish their own bylaws, compose a declaration of belief, and carry on certain minimal activities, their organization must be recognized as a church with all the perquisites enjoyed by the largest, wealthiest, and most powerful denominations in the U.S.

It is not necessary for a person to attend a seminary or other institution or to obtain a theological degree in order to qualify as a minister of the gospel. The Universal Life Church has ordained some 6 million persons under various titles—including bishops, cardinals, and Doctors of Divinity, for modest fees; and has chartered some 35,000 churches, each of which pays a monthly fee of $2.00 to the mother church in Modesto.

# Church and State

The First Amendment of our Constitution declares that Congress "shall make no law respecting an establishment of religion, or prohibiting the free exercise thereof . . ." More important words, in my opinion, have never been inscribed on paper or parchment or made the law of any nation.

Yet perhaps no others have evoked or occasioned more controversy.

At the same time, every candid or objective scholar or historian will acknowledge that this provision gave peace and harmony to the American people, even with a population committed to various religious ideologies, often deeply antithetical to one another. The sectarian wars, which had drowned Europe in blood and misery for centuries, were superseded in this blessed country by a harmonious separation of state from church, in which the latter was supported entirely by voluntary membership and contributions.

But then came those *betes noires,* the Internal Revenue Code and Service (IRS), which conferred a variety of exemptions and immunities upon churches and religious organizations. Until quite recently, the government made few or no attempts to interfere in any way with these privileges or advantages.

Then situations arose in which the IRS began flexing its muscles to demonstrate again that it does not exist primarily to collect taxes, but to exercise control, to oppress and destroy some, and to heap unparalleled favors upon others. When certain churches established their own schools—allegedly to avoid the terrible and destructive ordeals of forced busing to distant schools—the IRS was used to destroy them by declaring them "corporations for profit" unless they could meet a number of impossible requirements.

**NEW vs OLD**

In recent years, more or less as part of the tax resistance movement, a number of organizations, principally Rev. Kirby Hensley's Universal Life Church (ULC) and Jerome Daly's Basic Bible Church, have been ordaining ministers and organizing congregations in considerable numbers around the country for the purpose of reducing taxes by utilizing the immunities granted to religious organizations.

The ULC has won some strategic victories over the IRS; and actually many of its ministers and congregations meet the basic conditions for such advantages.

However, some of the old-line or established churches have shown fear and hatred for these newcomers. One prominent Methodist, who wrote a book giving his reasons why certain churches should enjoy tax exemptions, proposed that such immunities should not be granted to any organization until it was at least 20 and preferably 50 years old.

In its battle with these new entities, the IRS has issued a compendium of rules and regulations which have no real basis in its statute. For example, where this states that the member of a religious order will be exempt from income and Social Security taxation on any income received from work performed at the behest of his superior, the IRS now by regulation taxes even the salary of a Jesuit priest acting as chaplain in the U.S. Senate or the armed forces, even when ordered to do so by the general of his order.

At one time, many nuns and brothers who taught in the public schools were exempt from taxation on salaries so earned; now such immunity applies only if they teach in Catholic schools under orders from their superiors.

The problem of proliferating and non-traditional churches and religious organizations has given the IRS a huge headache. To combat them, one of its techniques is to send the officers of target churches long and detailed questionnaires, the answers to which would reveal more information than if a complete examination of books and records were conducted, which is strictly forbidden in Sec. 7605(c) of the IR Code.

However, under its assumed authority to determine whether an entity is really a church, it will, if the first questionnaire is answered in full, send another and then another, *ad infinitum*. And then it may:

● Conclude by declaring the church a "corporation for profit";

● Subject it to harrowing audits;

● Inform the state authorities that its properties must be fully taxed;

● Deny exemptions for contributions to it by members or the public; and then

● Invent other sanctions to make life miserable or impossible for it.

**LITTLE BASIS**

In all of this, the IRS creates its own laws, which have little or no base in the code itself. It conceives its duty to consist in a discriminatory application and enforcement of its regulations in order to make profits for some and to destroy others.

For example, I know of several perfectly viable churches and congregations, which have existed for many years and which have always met every requirement for exemptions and immunities, but which have incurred the wrath of the bureaucracy or some other powerful interest; these entities have been hounded and harassed beyond endurance.

On the other hand, I know of old, wealthy, and powerful religious organizations which have blatantly violated Sec. 501(c)(3), which provides the basis for their exemptions, and have done so not only with total impunity, but without so much as a word of warning or reprimand from the IRS.

# Social Security Obligations of Churches

First of all, members of recognized religious orders who have taken a vow of poverty are not required to enter the SS system (Sec. 501(d)). However, they may do so by election ("Regulation," No. 4, Subpart K, 404.1015(a)).

Secondly, ministers, priests, rabbis, members of religious orders who have not taken a vow of poverty and Christian Science practitioners will automatically come under the SS program as "self-employed" individuals unless they file Form 4361 during the first two-year period in which they receive income for service in such capacity.

If they waive SS **benefits,** the action is irrevocable. However, if such **an individual had filed a waiver of exemption** previous to 1967, he cannot leave the program.

(However, "An exemption which is effective with respect to a minister or a member of a religious order has no application to service performed by such minister or member which is not in the exercise of his ministry or in the exercise of duties required by such order" ("Income Tax Regulations as of June 29, 1978," v. 3, "Proposed Regulations," Sec. 1.1402(c)-5(a)(2), Commerce Clearing House). But note: "Exercise of his ministry" or "duties required" are not defined, just as government cannot define "religion.")

All such personnel are treated as "self-employed." So they are required to file their own returns and contribute to SS (Sec. 1402(e)).

But we should note that all such persons are entitled to a very important housing allowance (Sec. 107), which involves a substantial reduction in taxable income.

Another question has frequently arisen: Since Sec. 508(c) of the IRS Code states that "churches, their integrated auxiliaries and conventions or associations of churches" are not required to file for exemption, several have written to ask, "Why would anyone do so?" The best answer I can offer is that, by so doing, the organization will be listed in the "Cumulative Index of '170' Organizations" so that contributors may be certain that their contributions will be tax-deductible. However, by making such disclosure to the IRS, the organization may invite examination and harassment, which has occurred in a great many instances.

One minister wrote, asking whether a school operated as an activity of a church is an "integrated auxiliary" thereof. It seems obvious that it certainly is, and therefore enjoys a mandated exemption from filing anything with the IRS in order to enjoy full immunity to taxation or IRS surveillance.

This is my position: I see no pressing reason why a church would, or should, file any information with the IRS or make any request for exemption.

Interestingly enough, the 1979 "Publication 557" states specifically that religious schools enjoy the same immunity as do churches; however, "Publication 1023," which deals with the same subject, omits any reference to schools, *per se.*

If church schools established after 1960 to avoid busing are declared "racist," this could be an attempt by the IRS to place them in a category with corporations-for-profit and subject them to audits and intensive investigation.

# Clergy and IRS Form 4361

For years after the self-employed became subject to Social Security taxation, the ministers could not participate; then, for a time, they could do so only by affirmative action; but now they can be released only by filing Form 4361; however, under the law, **this must be done within two years of the first receipt of money in this capacity.**

Form 4029 may be filed by laymen who belong to a recognized group or church which rejects the entire philosophy of Social Security; but it is so worded that only the Amish can qualify.

**However, I recently met a man who maintains that any minister can file the 4361 to invalidate taxation on income from any source; and that any person who conscientiously opposes Social Security may file the 4029.** Then, when and if the IRS rejects the application, the citizen should sue the Agency in a United States District Court for refusal to grant equal protection under the laws, as mandated in the Fourteenth Amendment to the Constitution.

However, every ordained minster who receives a salary from his church has important advantages even if the IRS refuses to honor his request to be relieved from Social Security contributions. There are, in particular, two provisions in the code, placed there specifically for his benefit: Section 107 (Rental Value of Parsonages); and 119 (Meals and Lodging Furnished for the Convenience of the Employer).

Section 7605 is wonderfully protective of churches and ministers: it provides that even if a church is in violation of the law it s books may not be audited nor may anyone below the status of a Regional Commissioner (there are eight such officials) even take notice of the violation. Not only are the finances and income of the church free from taxation: they are also immune to disclosure to, or scrutiny by, anyone whatsoever.

Thus, not even the IRS can discover what a church does with its money, or what it pays its pastor or other employees, unless they reveal such facts themselves. Section 107 permits the church to give its minster a separate check, not includible in gross income and therefore not reportable, which will cover all expenses of maintaining his household, with the exception of food and personally paid servants.

In the case of a home owned by the minister, the check will cover utilities, repairs, painting, furniture, drapes, upkeep of every kind, and not only the interest but also the principal payments on a mortgage or purchase contract. The church can also supply an automobile to be used in parish work, as well as travel and many other incidental expenses. Of course, the minister is entitled to all the exemptions and allowances available to anyone else, in order to reduce the taxability of the remaining portion óf his income, given him by the church in a separate check.

Section 119 is especially tailored for clerics in certain churches where we frequently find bishops or priests who occupy rectories or other facilities owned by the church or by the bishop as a corporation sole in which this functionary is regarded as an agent of his employer, and where meals, lodging, servants, clothing, cars, and everything else is supplied on a totally tax-exempt basis, no matter what the standard of living may be.

**Although the ordinary minister in a Protestant denomination or an independent Bible church may not enjoy all these advantages, he can certainly and quite easily achieve exemption from taxation on an income of at least $20,000.**

# Conditions for Religious Immunity

I have often stated, and I now repeat, that the Internal Revenue Code and Service are not intended primarily as a method of collecting taxes. They are, instead, a vast system of extortion and bribery, having as their true objective, the control and regimentation of our people. They serve as a means of enriching some, while impoverishing others; they reward those who support the existing governmental structure and crush, or attempt to crush, all dissent thereto.

The First Amendment declares that Congress shall make no law respecting an establishment of religion or prohibiting the free exercise thereof. Yet, in obvious violation of this mandate, the Internal Revenue Code is studded with provisions which confer unparalleled financial advantages upon religious bodies and personnel **on condition that none of these engage in any political activity.** (It is true that this is not enforced against certain powerful entities.)

Thus bribed, almost all clerics and religious organizations not only abstain from criticism of federal atrocities—in fact, from any participation in the political process, in which churches could presumably be powerful influences for good. We can scarcely expect a minister who receives a salary of $30,000 which is exempt from income taxation and Social Security contributions to object to so beneficial a system; nor can we reasonably believe that an organization with a multi-million dollar income deriving from commercial sources, which is immune to both taxation and disclosure, will find any fault with this situation.

On the other hand, in spite of what the Constitution declares, if any religious group or organization dares voice dissent, the IRS stands ready, not merely to withdraw its immunities and advantages, but also to pounce upon it with a virulence and ferocity that one might think should be reserved for embezzlers, murderers, and rapists.

I could cite other cases in point, but in the following discussion I will focus on a single religious body—the Church of Scientology. Like Jefferson, I am not concerned with the tenets or practices of any religious group so long as these do not constitute a threat to society: that is none of my business, nor that of the government.

There is no question in my mind that this organization can qualify as a religious institution just as fully as can any one of a hundred or more of others, upon which the IRS confers its unqualified blessings.

The "crime" of Scientology is not to be found in its doctrines, discipline, or operation, but in the fact that it has dared to challenge and expose the operations of the federal colossus in a battle that now extends over some 25 years. The crimes committed by the government against this group are such as one might expect under a totally authoritarian regime, using extreme police measures to crush and destroy dissent.

The manner in which the IRS and other government agencies, including the FDA and the FBI, have violated the constitutional protections in their vendetta against the Scientologists as well as the basic provisions of law under which they operate, are sufficient to make an American wonder whether we are not already engulfed in the totalitarian state.

# IRS Attack on Private and Church Schools

When the IRS issued its devastating regulations intended to destroy all private schools (except the Jewish) established after 1957 or 1960, it must have had a premonition of massive protest; but we doubt that it realized what its extent would be. Remember that whereas the federal government now hands out $21 billion annually for aid to education in multi-form programs, these newer private schools—the object of its wrath—were not asking for a penny, only the privilege to exist as tax-exempt entities, for which they qualify under all existing law.

The arrogance and brutality of this government agency could scarcely be exceeded. Under its directive, all these schools would be required to:

• Enroll minority students equal in number at least to 20 percent of their ratio in the community;

• Actively recruit such students;

• Provide them with scholarships (intead of requiring them to pay tuition like all others);

• Hire teachers of minority races, whether qualified or not, and whether or not they desire such positions; and

• Actively promote racial integration in their schools and communities.

In short, they would have to hire totally undesirable pupils who would not wish to attend such schools which not only receive no public or federal funds but which are supported by tuition-payments which are not tax-deductible by the parents who send their children to them.

The reaction threw the IRS into confusion. Under pressure, it conducted a hearing at its own headquarters (not in a congressional building), at which several hundred indignant individuals, who travelled to Washington at their own expense, expressed their convictions and opinions in no uncertain terms. No one supported the IRS guidelines except the bureaucrats themselves.

As a result, at least temporarily, the IRS has pulled in its horns. According to an article released by the Associated Press on Feb. 10, 1979, the agency has now revised its "plans for fighting racial bias in private schools." It will now find somewhat different techniques by which to attack the 3,500 white academies set up in the South during the past 25 years. Its requirements—so we are told—will permit some degree of "flexibility" in determining whether or not the schools can retain tax-exempt status.

The outcome of this battle is fraught with enormous consequences. To what extent shall the IRS continue to exercise unlimited powers as the national instrument of extortion and bribery in order to place every man, woman, and child in the U.S. under the heel of its regimentation?

I have stated a thousand times that the primary purpose of the IRS is not to collect taxes, but to force federal controls upon the people; to bribe the obedient and destroy the dissidents; to enrich its favorites and to impoverish the independents. Nowhere is the truth of this statement more evident than in its attempt to destroy the private schools.

# IRS vs. New Churches

The proliferation of small churches poses a crucial problem for the IRS. Sometimes old-line denominations regard them as illegitimate and see in this development a threat to their advantages and immunities.

The fact is that even if a church is in violation of the law, no one below the status of a Regional Commissioner (of whom there are eight) may even take note thereof; and even he, under such circumstances, is prohibited from making an examination of its books (Section 7605). No church or association of churches is required to pay taxes or make any report to any one, including its own members.

Acutally, it is quite a simple matter to organize and establish a church: if so desired, a charter may be obtained from a mail-order entity, which will also supply instructions. It is only necessary that three persons, who will constitute the board of trustees, with appropriate titles, prepare articles of incorporation as required in their own state, have these routinely approved by the pertinent authority, and prepare the bylaws under which the corporation will operate.

The church will, of course, have a name and a simple declaration of belief or faith. Services will be held at stated times; the decisions of its board will be inscribed in its minutes. The church will have its own bank accounts and keep its financial records separate from those of any individual.

This church can be entirely independent, or it can be a branch of a denomination, such as the Universal Life Church. However, we should note that property belonging to a church cannot be legally transferred without adequate consideration to an individual or to any other entity except one having the same or similar status in the IR Code.

If the pastor of the new church wishes his home to become its sanctuary and pastorate, exempt from local property taxes, it will usually have to be deeded to the church; however, the assessor, as in Arizona, may refuse to grant exemption even when this is done.

It may be just as well not to deed such property to the church; and there are other extraordinary tax advantages which cannot be denied by the IRS. Under Section 170(b) of the code, the pastor may deduct up to 50 percent of his adjusted gross income received from outside sources, as a contribution to his church. Thus, if he earns $20,000, let us say, from a plumbing business, he can deduct $10,000 as a contribution to his church. The taxable portions of the remaining $10,000 may then be reduced by the same exemption and other deductions to which everyone is entitled.

But this is by no means all: under Section 107, he is entitled to a "housing allowance," which—paid to him in a separate check—covers taxes, repairs, upkeep, furniture, furnishings, utilities, rentals, and mortgage payments, all of which is excludable from gross income and therefore not reportable on Form 1040. No one except the minister and the board of trustees need know the amount of such payments.

The fact is that by becoming a minister and organizing a church, a family can easily enjoy a $20,000 income without owing any income taxes. And if the minister receives a salary from his church, he can file Form 4361—within two years after such income begins—and be excused from making contributions to Social Security.

It is estimated that tens of thousands of such church corporations are now in operation in the U.S., all enjoying the immunities and advantages described here.

# *Harassing Some Churches*

I have received detailed letters from ministers of various independent churches describing the harassment they are undergoing from the IRS. Although the agency admits that it has no authority to examine or audit the books of any church, it has demanded an answer to long lists of questions which would constitute a more complete disclosure than any audit could reveal.

One questionnaire demanded:

● Have you ever filed an application for recognition of exemption with the Internal Revenue Service? (This requirement is specifically waived in Sec. 508(c) of the Code.)

● Have you submitted a confirmed copy of your creating instruments and by-laws? (Such submission is made only to state authorities, and once granted by them, is beyond IRS authority.)

● Does your organization have a recognized creed and form of worship—explain in detail. (This does not concern the IRS in any way.)

● State how many members your church has; has any one been rejected for membership, and if so, on what ground? (No business of the IRS.)

● Provide a complete history of your church from the date of its founding. (This does not concern the IRS.)

● Provide a complete list of officers and directors, including a resume of backgrounds. (Not necessary.)

● Describe fully whether you pay compensation or make any other payment to or for individuals who perform services for your organization. (This is none of the government's business.)

● Identify contributors who have given $500 or more during your most recent accounting year. (The IRS has no authority to demand an answer to such a question.)

● Submit a complete schedule of receipts and expenditures. (This is precisely the kind of information which Sec. 7605 forbids the IRS from attempting to obtain from a church.)

To a church in Oklahoma, the IRS wrote a long letter demanding detailed information concerning its creed, beliefs, precepts, discipline, organizational structure, number of members, their voting rights, method of selection, etc. It also demanded copies of service bulletins, newsletters, a description of bookkeeping procedures, general ledgers, cash · receipt journal, bank statements, deposit slips, cancelled checks, complete summaries of income and expenses, together with a listing of assets and liabilities; also a roster of the 10 largest contributors and their relationship to the founders, elders, and ministers of the church.

Our suggestion to any church or pastor who receives a similar letter is to reply demanding that the IRS comply fully with its own law, as laid down in Sec. 7605; that it cite explicitly the provisions in the IR Code which confer the assumed authority; that it obey the provisions of the Privacy Act of 1974 by explaining the purpose of the questionnaire; what will be done with the information if obtained; what punishment can or will be inflicted upon the church or its pastor if such information is not supplied; whether a similar questionnaire is being sent to all churches in the US; and if not, why has this particular one been singled out for harassment and persecution.

In our opinion, in any such procedure as outlined herein, the IRS is bluffing.

# Church Harassment by the IRS

One of the "crimes" committed by the Church of Scientology consisted in publishing a few years ago a fat compilation of secret material called the "IRS Papers" which the agency had been forced to disgorge under court proceedings brought by Phil Long of Bellevue, Wash. But the war between the church and the federal government had begun long before that date.

The harassment suffered by the church, and recorded in a volume called "The American Inquisition," has continued almost without interruption since 1950. Government agents infiltrated and spied upon the organization, made secret tapes of discussions at meetings, monitored and opened its mail, and raided its offices in one city after another.

On January 4, 1963, the church headquarters in Washington, D.C., was invaded and looted by a small army of U.S. marshalls and deputized longshoremen, who roamed through the structure, entered bedrooms where couples were sleeping, and escorted by motorcycle policemen, carried away documents and other personal property which filled two large vans.

Pursuant to this atrocity, the church sued the government for a return of its property in a litigation that dragged on for more than 10 years. Finally, in October, 1973, after the United States Circuit Court of Appeals had declared the original raid unlawful, several tons of property were returned, including 5,000 bound volumes, 20,000 pamphlets, and 65 E-meters. However, the church was compelled to pay the cost of storage for its illegally seized property; nor was all of it returned or accounted for.

Anyone who believed that this experience would carry any weight with the IRS was soon to be rudely disabused. For in July 1977, by actual count, some 134 government agents burst into three headquarters buildings occupied by the church in Los Angeles and in Washington state. The pretext was that the church had infiltrated government agencies in an attempt to discover and copy documents pertaining to the church. The irony concerning this charge is, of course, that under the Freedom of Information Act, the government is under mandate to release all such materials to affected parties upon request.

It was said that the raids were prompted and justified by information received from a defecting church official, who, of course, was probably a federal agent planted within the church.

We note that—without offering any proof—the government charged the church with doing precisely what the government had been doing all along. There is no doubt that several hundred thousand dollars—perhaps millions—of taxpayer-funds have been spent in the ceaseless and criminal persecution of this church.

The raids were carried out by goons who used axes and sledge-hammers to batter down doors while officials of the church stood by, offering the invaders the key to the premises. Instead, property worth many thousands of dollars was destroyed; and tons of property, including many thousands of items of literature, were hauled away.

James J. Kilpatrick stated in his syndicated column of August 14, 1977, that a federal judge had already declared the July raid illegal and ordered the return of the seized property; but he observes also that the harassment suffered by the church has been terribly expensive. As in other situations, even if the IRS cannot prevail in court against victims, it hopes to bankrupt them and ruin their reputations so public sympathy will be lost and the financial support of members will be reduced.

# Ch. 8

## Universal Trust Plan, or Sensible Retirement

## 1981 Economic Recovery Act Evaluation

# *Universal Trust Plan*

The advantages to the people of the Universal Trust Plan over the existing Social Security system are so great as to render the two without comparison.

The UTP would put an end to the need for fractional reserve banking, since trust accounts for tens of millions of people would, in due course, provide 100 per cent reserves for all loans. Banks would no longer create credit based on government bonds in ratios determined by the Federal Reserve Board of Governors.

At present, in a swindle that almost defies comprehension, banks obtain federal bonds for nothing, collect heavy interest on them from the taxpayers and then use them to create loans on deposits up to ten times the value of the bonds. On all this heavy interest is collected and guaranteed by solid collateral.

Under the UTP, there could never again be any manipulation of credit or currency; and never again could there be inflation, deflation, panics, or depression. At the present time, under the Federal Reserve system, private bankers collect more than $300 billion a year in interest on credit created out of thin air.

Under the UTP, the great bulk of the money would go to the millions of working Americans while building their own estates. Banking and investment institutions would become, like the present savings and loan associations, simple managers of depositors' funds, a service for which they would receive a fee of perhaps 1 or 1.5 per cent of the income derived from those investments.

The SS system, which now has 55,000 employees and costs about $2 billion for administration alone, would be abolished; everything that it now does and much more would be performed gladly and expertly by private institutions without cost to depositors or recipients of pension or annuity funds.

The UTP would remove the federal bureaucracy forever from an activity in which it should never have been involved.

The UTP will provide ample funds at reasonable cost for every conceivable type of sound investment and so ensure the constant growth and secure expansion in every phase of our economy.

Along with the termination of the SS system, the federal income tax will also be abolished. These two steps alone will reduce the federal bureaucracy by some 135,000 and its cost by approximately $10 billion. Furthermore, the savings to the taxpayers because they will no longer have to pay the cost of making income tax returns and fighting the IRS may save them an additional $3 or $4 billion.

It should be emphasized that the UTP will contain provisions by which retirees can take much better care of dependents and survivors than is the case under the present SS. Anyone who builds an estate of $400,000 and can thus draw $2,500 a month without even touching the principal, can certainly provide the best care for survivors. Furthermore, since most of those who suffer disability will already have created trusts of considerable size, they also will have enough to care for their own needs.

Of course, as is now the case, there will always be some who have neither assets nor income; such individuals will have to be cared for by private or public charity.

At present, the greatest tragedy that could befall the SS system or its contributors would be an average increased longevity of 10 or 12 years. It is well known to the actuarial profession that should a cure be found for cancer and should the incidence of heart failure be drastically reduced, the burden upon SS would simply become insupportable.

Under the UTP, the general health and lengthening of lives of retirees would be among the greatest of blessings; for their retirement would cost neither the government nor the younger generations anything; on the contrary, the contributions and the consumer market supplied by older people would be of incalculable benefit to society. Thus, with Browning, we could joyfully declare that "the best is yet to be, the last of life, for which the first was made."

Most of all, the UTP will create a totally different society, one consisting of tens of millions of free, self-reliant individuals, secure in their economic and political lives.

# *Economic Recovery Tax Act*

In this and in subsequent articles, I analyze and evaluate the Reagan Economic Recovery Tax Act of 1981.

As will be demonstrated in the next article, rates of taxation on given income will be reduced. However, the administration is expecting not smaller, but increased revenues, which it hopes will result from greater prosperity and business activity.

We were also told that the budget would be balanced by 1983 or 1984—a pledge similar to that made, but flagrantly violated, by the Carter administration.

At first, Reagan promised a deficit not exceeding $42 billion for 1982; but now this seems to have been thrown into the "discard." It may be safe to say that the deficit will be $70 or $80 billion, with a rate of inflation which will approximate that for fiscal 1980 and 1981.

Furthermore, while the last Carter budget was about $640 billion—the one he proposed for 1982 was $749 billion—the Reagan official expenditures were pegged at $695 billion, an increase of $55 billion over the final Carter level. Where the Reagan administration got its figure, I do not profess to know.

As of now, our opinion is that total tax revenues will probably increase—as expected—in 1982, 1983 and 1984. However, this will be due, I believe, far more to the continuing inflation than to increasing business prosperity.

Nevertheless, let us hope for the best. I do not doubt that had the Carter-Mondale ticket received a strong mandate, with a cooperative Congress, by 1984 or 1985 the federal budget would be reaching $1 trillion and the national debt nearly $2 trillion. The purchasing power of the dollar would, meanwhile, probably plummet to about 5 cents.

The Recovery Tax Act provides for a 5 percent cut across the board in income taxes beginning October 1, and a 10-percent reduction in 1982 and 1983. According to the official computations printed in the explanation of the act, the lower tax rates will save taxpayers:

| Billions | Year |
| --- | --- |
| $1.565 | 1981 |
| 37.656 | 1982 |
| 92.732 | 1983 |
| 149.303 | 1984 |
| 199.974 | 1985 |
| 267.627 | 1986 |

Since this is a total of $748.9 billion less than would have been due without the Tax Recovery Act, it is obvious that such quantities of money left in the hands of private individuals over a six-year period will surely exercise a significant impact upon the social and economic life of the U.S.

We should note here that the rates of taxation are not the only reductions. Perhaps even more important and beneficial are various provisions dealing with gifts and estates and especially the new "unlimited marital deduction," all of which I will discuss in due course.

I venture one additional thought at this point: Had it not been for the burgeoning tax rebellion, you can be quite certain that there would have been no such enactment as the Economic Recovery Act of 1981—which is now offered to mollify, in some degree, the anger and frustration of the American taxpayers.

# How to Revitalize Our Government

In fiscal 1980, the cost of maintaining the federal bureaucracy—including retirement and fringe benefits—will be at least $75 billion; and the interest on the federal debt nearly $60 billion—a total of about $135 billion. When we realize that the personal federal income tax produced only $153 billion in 1977, it becomes obvious that almost all of this sum is consumed simply to support those excrescences on the body politic and to pay the interest on a debt resulting largely from wild deficit spending in peacetime, all perpetrated for the purpose of bribing enough people to vote for the present administration so that it can perpetuate itself in office, tax the middle class into poverty and destroy the American system of economy and government.

Actually, of course, the inflationary process has also largely repudiated the national debt. If an individual were, let us say, to borrow 10 bushels of potatoes, each weighing 50 pounds, and then, sometime later, declare that bushels had been reduced in amount to 5 pounds, and offer to settle the debt by repayments in such quantities, he would be engaged in exactly the same swindle now used by the federal government.

It sold 25-year bonds 20 years ago which paid 3 percent interest and received for them federal reserve notes which could be redeemed for good silver dollars or by foreigners in gold at $35 an ounce. Now those same bonds can be sold only at huge discounts; and the federal reserve notes received for them are worth less than one-fourth of what a dollar would buy when the bonds were sold.

Any businessman who operated in that way would be subject to a prison sentence.

But to return to the cost of the federal government, especially its

---

**Potential Savings in Federal Government:**

|  |  | Billions |
|---|---|---|
| 1. | By eliminating its own income and SS taxes | $100 |
| 2. | By requiring federal workers to fund their own retirement programs, as do those who are on Social Security | 14 |
| 3. | By terminating educational subsidies | 16 |
| 4. | By ending Revenue Sharing | 10 |
| 5. | By terminating research grants | 80 |
| 6. | By eliminating fraudulent claims and unnecessary programs in HEW | 30 |
| 7. | By eliminating overlapping programs | 25 |
| 8. | By reducing the size of the federal bureaucracy | 25 |
|  | **TOTAL** | $300 |

bureaucracy and debt: if this nation is to survive as a representative republic, both must be drastically reduced. Instead of continuing to increase this debt via deficit spending—which automatically requires additional billions in interest every year—this burden must be lightened. Furthermore, a great multitude of overlapping and unconstitutional programs must be curtailed or consolidated and many of their activities terminated.

By this process alone, we believe that at least $25 billion could be cut from the federal budget.

Whatever useful work federal bureaucrats do, beyond their constitutional mandate, should be turned over forthwith to the states as rapidly as possible or expedient. We believe that the savings possible as a result would be at least $25 billion.

Let us then summarize some of the savings which could be achieved in the federal government, even without abolishing many of its programs, but assuming the termination of the Internal Revenue Service and the Social Security Administration (to be replaced by a Universal Trust Plan). The bureaucracies which now administer these two agencies alone cost the taxpayers about $10 billion a year.

I emphasize that even this is by no means all that could be done. If the federal government were restricted to its constitutional mandate, its only activities would be those listed in Art. I, Sec. 8 of the Constitution, all of which deal with our relations to foreign states and to the interrelationships among our own states.

When this is done, we will have a constitutional republic again; and it would operate at perhaps one-third of the cost and manpower now projected by those at the top of the present administration. With the kind of government we advocate, not only would there be no deficit spending; the federal establishment could begin to make significant payments to reduce the national debt.

Finally, it should be noted that while our proposals contemplate the immediate termination of personal, corporate and Social Security taxation, federal obligations to its retirees would have to be met fully, as they could easily be through the sale of the U.S. power grid and various other assets; and, if necessary, by the imposition of a small and temporary general transactions tax, the cost of which to consumers would be slight compared to that involved in income and SS taxation. We believe that within 15 years, the SS system could be phased out completely and replaced by a Universal Trust Plan (UTP), which would return four or five times as much to every retiree for each dollar invested therein.

This would be the greatest socio-economic revolution of modern times; it would also be the most beneficial.

# Rate Reductions

Although there was a bitter battle in Congress between Democrats and Republicans over the amount of rate reductions to be established and when they should take effect, they seem not to have merited such attention and acrimony.

For example, for a married couple with $5,500 of taxable income, their liability in 1980 was $294. It will be $252 in 1982; $231 in 1983 and thereafter, a total reduction of $63, or 21 percent.

If their taxable income stands at $20,000, the tax was $3,273 in 1980; and will be $2,937 in 1981, $2,644 in 1983, and $2,497 thereafter. However, if inflation pushes the income to $24,600 in 1983, the tax will be $3,656, or almost $400 more than it was in 1980.

Of course, it must be understood that many taxpayers having the incomes shown in the accompanying table may have deductions, allowances and exclusions sufficient to offset all income tax liability. The table applies explicitly to those who use simply the zero deduction without itemizing; it applies also, of course, to any incomes remaining after all itemized deductions have been subtracted.

## TABLE SHOWING TAXES FOR DIFFERENT YEARS

### MARRIED COUPLES FILING JOINTLY

| Taxable Income | 1980 | 1982 | 1983 | 1984 | % Reduction |
|---|---|---|---|---|---|
| $20,200 | $ 3,273 | $ 2,937 | $ 2,644 | $ 2,497 | 23.4 |
| 60,000 | 19,678 | 17,705 | 16,014 | 15,168 | 22.9 |
| 85,600 | 33,502 | 30,249 | 27,278 | 25,920 | 25.7 |

### FOR SINGLE PERSONS

| Taxable Income | 1980 | 1982 | 1983 | 1984 | % Reduction |
|---|---|---|---|---|---|
| $ 3,400 | $ 154 | $ 132 | $ 121 | $ 121 | 21.4 |
| 15,000 | 2,605 | 2,330 | 2,097 | 2,001 | 23.2 |
| 41,500 | 13,392 | 12,068 | 10,913 | 10,319 | 29.5 |

The rates and reductions vary slightly for heads of households. For married couples with two substantial incomes, a long-needed reform has been established: The one with the smaller income may deduct from taxable income 5 percent thereof up to $1,500 in 1982 and 10 percent, up to $3,000, in 1983.

One of the most important changes in income tax rates is the fact that the highest will not exceed 50 percent on any form of individual revenue. Formerly, the maximum rate was 50 percent on earned and 70 percent on unearned income, such as dividends, interest, rentals, trust distributions, royalties etc. Now the maximum rate—50 percent—is the same for passive or unearned income from investments as from wages, salaries or self-employment income.

No doubt these reductions will be highly beneficial for taxpayers during the ensuing years and, in combination, will cut tax liability by many billions of dollars.

**INDEXING**

At this point, we should note that, beginning in fiscal 1985, the zero, i.e., the unitemized, deduction and all exemption-allowances will be indexed to keep pace with ongoing inflation. Since we now have a zero deduction of $2,400 for single persons, $3,400 for couples, and personal exemptions of $1,000 for dependents, if the rate of inflation in 1985 is 10 percent, these amounts will rise to $2,640, $3,740 and $1,100 respectively.

Note also that after years of pressure and controversy, churches and other ''charities'' have finally been able to make their influence felt. Since those who do not itemize gain nothing by making charitable contributions, these 501(c) organizations hope to profit by an amendment to Sec. 170, which now provides that in 1982 and 1983, 25 percent of charitable contributions totaling $100 will be deductible without itemizing. The same percentage will apply on a total of $300 in 1984; 50 percent of that amount in 1985; and the entire amount of contribution in 1986, when the provision expires in anticipation of a new amendment.

**CAPITAL GAINS**

Extremely important is a provision which, as of June 9, 1981, reduces the maximum tax on capital gains (and other forms of unearned income) from 70 to 50 percent. Thus a taxpayer who has a capital gain of $100,000 cannot be taxed at a ratio exceeding 50 percent of $40,000; $60,000 is exempt.

However, amounts in excess of $10,000 are still subject to the preference tax of 15 percent; thus, if a taxpayer has a capital gain of $100,000, the amount of tax due can be no more than $20,000, of which one-half will be subject to the 15 percent preference tax of $1,500.

Finally, the act amends Sec. 911 of the IR Code by increasing the amount of tax-free income Americans may receive while working abroad to $75,000 in 1982, $80,000 in 1983, $85,000 in 1984, $90,000 in 1985 and $95,000 in 1986 and thereafter. In addition, such employees may expend up to 16 percent of income received by those with a GS-14 status, as a tax-deductible item. In short, all the foreign representatives of the government (and others also) are now to enjoy a virtually tax-exempt way of life.

# *Friendly Legislation*

As we study the Recovery Tax Act, it becomes evident that those who conceived it are more friendly to the American middle class than any other administration since 1932. This is especially true because of the provisions dealing with gift and estate taxation.

The exemptions permitted in the sale of homes have been increased. Sec. 1034(c) of the IR Code has been amended to provide that the period between the sale of one home and the purchase of another, without tax liability on the sale of the first, has been increased from 18 to 24 months.

**Furthermore, Sec. 121(b) is** amended to provide that in the case of a homeowner who has attained the age of 55 and has lived in his principal domicile during three of the last five years, he or she or spouses will be permitted a once-in-a-lifetime non-taxable gain on the sale of such domicile of $125,000—an increase of $25,000 over the previous exemption.

Sec. 219 is amended to provide that non-taxable contributions to an Individual Retirement Account (IRA) are increased from $1,500 to $2,000 a year. A spousal IRA is increased from $1,750 to $2,250. **Perhaps even more important than the increase in the amount that may be** contributed is the fact that anyone, no matter whether covered or not by another annuity or pension system, may now establish his own IRA.

Sec. 404(c) is amended to permit self-employed individuals to increase their maximum tax-exempt contributions to their own (Keogh) retirement plans from 15 percent of $50,000, or $7,500, to 15 percent of $100,000, or $15,000.

One of the most valuable provisions in the new law will enable middle-class individuals to preserve their savings to a greater extent than before:

**New Gift Credits and Estate Exemptions**

| YEAR | CREDITS | EXEMPTIONS |
|---|---|---|
| 1982 | $ 62,800 | $225,000 |
| 1983 | 79,300 | 275,000 |
| 1984 | 96,000 | 325,000 |
| 1985 | 121,800 | 400,000 |
| 1986 | 155,800 | 500,000 |
| **After 1986** | 192,800 | 600,000 |

**Thus, beginning in 1986, anyone** can make a gift or bequest to anyone of $600,000 without taxation.

Sec. 2056 of the IR Code, as now amended, provides for an unlimited marital exemption: That is, when one spouse dies, the survivor can receive the entire estate, no matter how large, without federal tax liability. Since wives normally outlive their husbands by quite a number of years, this will be golden news to millions of women.

Sec. 2030(a)(2) now provides that closely held business estates, such as farms or city businesses, will be exempt from estate taxation by meeting certain requirements up to a value of $600,000 in 1981, $700,000 in 1982 and $750,000 in 1983 and thereafter.

Sec. 2503(b) provides that any number of non-taxable—actually unreported—gifts can be made to any number of other persons in amounts of $10,000 annually, an increase from $3,000.

I consider the provisions summarized in this article by far the most beneficial in the Recovery Tax Act.

# Recovery Encouraging

The Economic Recovery Tax Act fills almost 200 pages of fine print—in addition to which there are 90 pages of explanations. Many of these provisions are highly technical and apply only to corporations or individuals who have experts to explain them. We cannot take the space here to summarize these, which deal with cost-recovery programs, utility companies, windfall profits, tax straddles and other complicated matters of limited impact.

Nevertheless, a number of miscellaneous amendments have wide applicability, such as the following:

● Sec. 44A is amended to provide that the amounts which may be deducted from taxable income to pay for day-care so that taxpayers can pursue gainful employment outside the home are increased in some cases from $2,000 to $2,400 and in others from $4,000 to $4,800.

● Sec. 172(b)(6) is amended to provide that net operating losses may be carried forward for 15 instead of seven years.

● Sec. 46(a)(2)(A) is amended to permit increased deductions for rehabilitating 30- and 40-year-old buildings.

● Sec. 11(b) is amended to give small corporations a lower tax rate.

● Sec. 170(b)(2) is amended to permit an increase from 5 to 10 percent for charitable contributions by corporations.

● Sec. 274(b)(1)(C) is amended to permit employers to deduct from their taxable income the value of gifts to employees not exceeding $400.

● Sec. 128 is redesignated as Sec. 129 and a new Sec. 128 is added which provides that on a joint return up to $2,000 of interest paid a couple by a savings and loan association may be exempt from income taxation on certain savings certificates issued between September 30, 1981 and January 1, 1983, provided the yield on these does not exceed 70 percent of the average yield for the most recent auction of U.S. treasury bills which mature in 52 weeks. Such S&L certificates must be available in denominations of $500.

We suggest that readers study carefully this and the three preceding articles; understanding their contents could mean saving many thousands of dollars. If you work for wages or salary—even if you are already covered by some annuity plan—we suggest you establish your own Individual Retirement Account (IRA), which can be handled by almost any bank, trust company, or savings and loan association. This could reduce your current income taxes substantially, and create an irrevocable estate or retirement trust, which would keep you in comfort when you reach the age of 59½ or shortly thereafter; or constitute a wonderful bequest for heirs or devisees.

Since it always has been a principal objective of Liberty Lobby to help middle class Americans protect their assets and thus survive as proponents of responsible and republican government, we know of no better way to accomplish this.

# Ch. 9

# Jefferson, the Fed and the Financiers

# Founders' Objectives

Our Founding Fathers were determined to accomplish two objectives:

● The federal government should have exclusive power to issue currency;

● This currency should consist of, or be redeemable in, specie.

For this reason, they provided that Congress alone shall have the right to coin (issue) money and regulate the value thereof; and that no state should make anything except gold and silver coin a tender in the payment of debt.

This means, of course, that the currency must be issued by the Treasury; and that fiat bills of credit or money shall be banned forever.

Thomas Jefferson fought one of his most bitter and memorable battles over this crucial issue with Alexander Hamilton. The latter wanted and was able to establish a banking system basically similar to today's Federal Reserve. It was approved by congressional action and was given the power to issue currency, to expand or contract credit and thus to create inflation or deflation at will. This was what the financiers of that day—like those of the present—desired. By it, they made fabulous fortunes; and, as Jefferson declared, created an aristocracy based on moneyed interests.

## SIMPLE SOLUTION

Jefferson had a very simple solution for the monetary problem, which, had it been adopted, would have made the U.S. the most secure, peaceful and prosperous nation ever known. Had it been adopted, any emergency, and even the expenses of a great war, could have been met without borrowing money or increasing the taxes.

He proposed that

● The Treasury issue all currency;

● It consist of, or be redeemable in, specie; and

● During a war or other emergency, Congress issue interest-bearing notes in small denominations, which would be universally acceptable, either for savings or exchange, and which would be redeemed in specie and destroyed when the emergency was over.

Hamilton's First United States Bank was established in 1791, with a 20-year franchise. However, in 1811, President James Madison vetoed the attempt to renew its charter, and there was no national bank until 1816, when the Second United States Bank, also with a 20-year life, was established because of the debts created by the Second War with England (War of 1812).

The attempt to renew its charter was vetoed by Andrew Jackson in 1832. The national debt was liquidated in 1835.

## GREENBACKS

Since the people were so suspicious of any central banking authority, there was no such institution between 1836 and 1863—only state-chartered banks. Some 12,000 different currencies circulated during this period, many of them actually counterfeit.

However, the cost of the Civil War—when Lincoln issued $450 million in fiat greenbacks—brought on a new crisis, and the financiers were able to force through Congress the National Banking Act of 1863, whch gave them much of the power they craved.

Under this, the bankers could buy government bonds with greenbacks at face value, even though the greenbacks were purchased by them at 30 cents on the dollar. The bonds were redeemable in specie. The bankers then collected 7 percent interest in gold on the bonds.

When Lincoln had tried to borrow money, the financiers demanded interest at the rate of 28 percent. So, in spite of the tax- and interest-free greenbacks, they obtained at least that rate of return on most of what became the national debt at the close of the Civil War.

# Jefferson: Enemy of the Financiers

In 1791, Alexander Hamilton and his colleagues succeeded in establishing the First United States Bank, with a 20-year franchise.

Thomas Jefferson and James Madison, together with some of their allies, fought against it with all the power and logic at their disposal. They declared that it was not only unnecessary, but also un-Constitutional.

The Federalists, who had a majority in the Congress, under the leadership of Hamilton, were able to dominate the thinking of President George Washington, who did not understand the mysteries of finance.

In 1811, Madison vetoed the attempt to extend the life of the First United States Bank. However, as a result of the debts created by the Second War with England in 1812-14, he was forced to agree to the establishment of the Second U.S. Bank.

Although both of these banks were created by congressional statute and much of their capital came from 'the public purse, they were privately controlled and operated solely for private profit.

Jefferson assumed the presidency in 1801. He was an avowed enemy of the financiers, the bureaucrats and all Federalist attempts to subvert the Constitution. He fired the commissioner of internal revenue and his entire staff of agents; cut taxes by fully 50 percent and was still able to pay off almost half of the national debt in eight years. No wonder his administration was called a disaster by the spokesmen for the moneylenders. It was indeed that for the bankers of the Eastern seaboard and their European allies.

However, the expenses of the Second War with England increased the national debt from $45 million in 1812 to $127 million in 1816. The bankers loaned depreciated currency to the government, but collected both interest and principal in specie.

Jefferson wrote extensively concerning the monetary question. He proposed a plan by which the entire debt could be liquidated and the government be enabled to fight any war in the future or meet any emergency without increasing taxes or borrowing any money. He declared that the Constitution should be amended to prohibit forever any deficit spending. But this was bitterly opposed by the financiers, who grew rich as a result of wars, debts, taxes and onerous rates of interest.

Both the First and the Second U.S. Banks were basically similar to our present Federal Reserve System.

Under the statutes creating them, they were legally permitted to issue currency up to three times their specie reserves. However, they paid little attention to this restriction and issued far greater quantities when they wished to do so.

Before 1819, they promoted easy money and inflation, under which prices for goods at least quadrupled. During this period, the farmers borrowed to improve their freeholds.

Then, in the fall of 1819, credit was withdrawn, loans were called and a terrible agricultural depression followed, similar to that of 1920-21. Hundreds of thousands of farmers were foreclosed, and Jefferson himself might have been evicted from Monticello had not friends come to his aid.

Thus the bankers ruled supreme under the first two national banks. They used them to extort exorbitant interest from the government and the people. They crushed almost all opposition. But then the great populist Andrew Jackson, who was elected in 1828, vetoed the attempt to renew the franchise of the bank in 1832.

In 1835, the national debt was liquidated. There was no central bank at all between 1836 and 1863.

# Jefferson Was Right

If our national government had operated during the last 70 years on the principles laid down by Thomas Jefferson, this would indeed be a different country, and the dreadful alternatives now facing our people would not exist.

He declared in a letter to John Taylor, on November 26, 1798, that he wished one more amendment could be added to the Constitution—namely, one that would prohibit the government from borrowing money. (Incidentally, there is such a law in Singapore and South Korea, and in several of our states.)

To Samuel Kercheval, Jefferson wrote, under the date of July 12, 1816:

> **I consider the fortunes of our republic as depending, in an eminent degree, on the extinguishment of the public debt before we engage in any war; because, that done, we shall have revenue enough to improve our country in peace and defend it in war, without recurring either to new taxes or loans.**
>
> **But should this debt once more be swelled to a formidable size, its entire discharge will be despaired of, and we shall be committed to the English career of debt, closing with revolution. The discharge of the debt, therefore, is vital to the destinies of our government.**

In a series of letters written in 1813 to his son-in-law, John W. Eppes, he outlined in detail his proposals by which the federal government could conduct even the most expensive war without imposing any new taxes or borrowing any money whatever.

But, since this was not what the financiers or the so-called liberal politicians wanted, they have conspired to plunge this nation into a debt so great that it simply staggers the imagination. The politicians buy votes by spending money, which creates the debt, and the financiers collect interest on it in perpetuity.

The producing taxpayers are the unsung victims. It now costs more than $100 billion a year just to pay the interest on the debt, which increases enormously every year, even in peacetime. During 1982-83, the deficit is expected to exceed $150 billion. It also costs the taxpayers at least $100 billion a year simply to maintain the federal bureaucracy.

The fact is, that even though a national government can, for a time, stave off collapse by deficit spending, there is a point at which this becomes impossible and bankruptcy supervenes. When people will no longer buy government bonds or when sufficient taxes cannot be collected to finance the deficits by paying the interest on the debt, this situation will have arrived.

Of course, government can do, and does, a number of things not available to a private individual or corporation, whose remaining assets, when bankrupt, become subject to seizure by creditors.

In greater extremity, it can repudiate the entire debt, making its securities absolutely worthless—something that has happened again and again in history. Or the government can freeze or block the transfer or redemption of its debt, or impose moratoriums, delays or other conditions on the scheduled payment of interest or the repayment of principal.

When Jefferson became president, he faced a situation moving in the direction where we have now arrived. He abolished the Internal Revenue Service, fired all the tax collectors, reduced taxes by 50 percent, and paid off nearly half the national debt in eight years.

Oh, for Jeffersonians in the White House and on Capitol Hill! But to send them there, we will first have to rid ourselves of the oligarchy, which rules this country principally through the operation of the Federal Reserve System. Have the American people the knowledge, and the capacity for organization, necessary to accomplish this objective? Our fate hangs in the balance.

# *Rational Proposals*

In 1813, Thomas Jefferson wrote a series of letters to his son-in-law John W. Eppes, chairman of the House Finance Committee. In these missives, Jefferson dealt with the monetary question (as he did in various other epistles).

Briefly stated, his proposals were that:
● The national debt should be extinguished as rapidly as possible and never permitted to exist again.
● Only the general government should be empowered to issue currency, minted or in any form.
● This should be redeemable in specie, if not originally in that form.
● During a period of war or other emergency, the government should issue, to whatever extent necessary, a medium of exchange consisting of interest-bearing bills of credit, similar to those the Continental Congress issued between 1781 and 1788;
● Even if some inflation might result, non-interest-bearing bills should be issued during such emergency. All, however, would be redeemed in specie when the emergency was over; and
● Once the general government was free of debt, an amendment should be added to the Constitution permitting the government to allocate surplus funds to the states for the purpose of establishing libraries, schools and institutions of higher learning, as well as other facilities that can serve the general welfare.

Had these proposals been adopted, the financiers would have been defeated, and this nation would have had an entirely different history.

As we have already noted, Andrew Jackson vetoed the attempt to extend the franchise of the Second United States Bank. This should have been a golden opportunity to establish the kind of monetary system proposed by Jefferson. But the financiers were still powerful enough to prevent it. Furthermore, the people were deeply suspicious of any central banking authority, even a Constitutional one.

Because of their defeat by Jackson, the financiers punished the American people by contriving the terrible panic of 1837, in which thousands of farmers lost their freeholds.

Then, between 1836 and 1863, there was no central bank at all—only state-chartered institutions, which could issue their own currency. They were supposed to redeem this paper money in specie, on demand. There were some 12,000 banks of issue.

At the time, about 5,000 different kinds of currency in circulation were either fraudulent or actually counterfeit, as Charles Beard explains in his monumental "Rise of American Civilization." Thus, many recipients of currency could not know whether it had any value or would be redeemed by the issuing institution.

However, since most of the money used in exchanges consisted of silver coin minted by the treasury, the nation bumped along in this way for nearly 30 years. The financiers awaited their next golden opportunity to achieve their objectives—or at least some of them—during the crisis created by the Civil War.

# Money Is Power

During the early years of our republic, a titanic struggle was waged between the financial interests, led by Alexander Hamilton, on the one hand, and by the populist republicans on the other, led by Jefferson, Madison and Franklin.

This conflict resulted in a kind of compromise, in which the Jeffersonians were able to establish a substantially Constitutional government. But the financiers won strategic victories, including the creation of the First United States Bank. Although they have suffered some defeats—especially under Andrew Jackson—they have never been subdued or placed under a proper Constitutional regimen.

### CENTRAL BANKS

The Second United States Bank was established in 1816. Under both of these institutions and partially under the National Banking Act of 1863, the financiers achieved basic and far-reaching powers to control our society, our economy and our political structures.

However, it was only with the passage of the Federal Reserve Act in 1913 and the elaboration of its powers by amendments thereto under Franklin Delano Roosevelt that the international bankers finally achieved the total sovereignty which had been their aim from the beginning.

At this point, let us note that, under the now-existing monetary system, the Fed has power to:

● Inflate or deflate the currency at will;

● Create panics or depressions by scientific procedures;

● Set interest rates; and

● Determine who shall have credit or what the money supply shall be.

It operates in tandem with the Internal Revenue Service (IRS) to finance wars, to create astronomical debts for the nation and to impose onerous taxes upon the people.

Actually, we can regard Congress and the Federal Reserve as cognate bodies and thus, when we refer to one, include the other in the reference. There is a complete union between them, the elected representatives of the people acting merely and simply as the instrument to carry out the will of the financiers.

### FINANCIERS

And who are these? Among others, we may mention the Rockefellers; Chase Manhattan Bank; Kuhn-Loeb and Company; J. P. Morgan interests; Rothschilds and Warburgs of England, France and Germany.

There are others—legions of others—allies and servants who are well paid for their services. The financiers' objectives are achieved by bribing those who can be bribed or are worth bribing. Others are intimidated or made the recipients of subsidies; still others receive special tax advantages as long as they are obedient. The media are owned outright or under their control. The vast masses of people are subjected to propaganda so clever and deceitful that little understanding or rebellion is likely to be found among them.

Only the great independent middle class remains a potential bulwark against them, for its millions of members cannot be bribed, subsidized or deceived entirely. We have, therefore, a war between them and the federal government, especially the IRS, which is an instrument of the financiers, operating to harass, bankrupt and destroy the independent entrepreneurs. The final outcome of this battle will determine the fate of this nation and that of the entire Western World.

# Fed Conspiracy

Of all the legislation ever passed by our Congress, the Federal Reserve Act involved more deceit and conspiracy than any other.

In preparation for it, Congress passed the Aldrich-Vreeland Emergency Currency Act of 1908, which, among other things, created a National Monetary Commission consisting of 16 handpicked congressmen. Under the leadership of Sen. Nelson Aldrich, they toured Europe in 1909 at a cost of $500,000, supposedly searching for monetary information.

Understandably, they arrived at a consensus that America should establish a monetary system similar to the ones existing in England, France and Germany.

In November, 1909, a group of bankers and their expert advisers, led by Aldrich, boarded a private car at a railroad station in Hoboken, New Jersey, bound on a mission so secret that it was years before any facts concerning it were revealed to the public. Among those who attended were:

● A. Piatt Andrew, assistant secretary of the treasury;

● Frank Vanderlip, president of the National City Bank of New York, who represented the Rockefeller interests as well as those of Kuhn-Loeb and Company;

● Henry P. Davison of Morgan and Company;

● Charles D. Norton of the First National Bank of New York;

● Benjamin Strong, Wall Street manipulator; and

● A number of others, representing the most powerful banking interests in the U.S.

However, the most interesting member of the entourage was probably Paul Moritz Warburg, who had come to America from Germany in 1902. With $500,000 of Rothschild money, Warburg had purchased a partnership in Kuhn-Loeb and Company. He had been on an indefinite leave of absence with an annual salary of $500,000, while traveling America promoting the concept of a great, privately owned and privately controlled monetary system, to be established by congressional statute.

**BANKING SAFARI**

This banking safari was bound for Jekyll Island, off the coast of mainland Georgia. There, during conferences lasting two weeks, they hammered out the provisions they wished to include in a package of monetary legislation. The result was the Aldrich plan, introduced into Congress on January 16, 1911.

It enjoyed the support of President William Taft, but reeked so strongly of Wall Street that its defeat was a foregone conclusion. It never even got out of committee.

It was the wily and cunning alien Paul Warburg who engineered the passage of the "Federal Reserve Act"—a title that he suggested to deceive the people and the members of Congress into thinking the act would establish a governmental institution. Prof. Henry Parker Willis from the (Rockefeller) University of Chicago was drafted by the Carter-Glass House Committee on Finance to prepare the text of the proposed legislation—a story told in great detail in a book he published in 1923.

The enactment of the Federal Reserve law required a degree of deceit and conspiracy scarcely equaled elsewhere in American history. The bill's proponents declared that the Federal Reserve System would:

● Be an agency of the government;

● Establish a solid monetary system;

● Prevent forever the recurrence of panics or depressions;

● Make inflation or deflation impossible; and

● Provide all necessary funds for business activity.

Charles Augustus Lindbergh was the father of the "Lone Eagle." He was also a congressman from Minnesota. Lind-

bergh seems to have been the only individual who fully understood the nature of the conspiracy behind the legislation. He declared that it would constitute a scientific basis for the creation of depressions or inflation at will. He did not live long thereafter.

**REMOVING TAFT**

Since Taft had approved the proposed legislation, it was necessary to remove him from the political scene. Therefore the bankers found their pliant tool in the flamboyant hypocrite Woodrow Wilson, who was nominated for the presidency by the Democratic Party in 1912.

However, since the Republicans were then in the majority, Theodore Roosevelt was recruited to organize the Bull Moose Party and thus split the Republican vote.

Both Wilson and Roosevelt, financed by the bankers, went up and down the United States denouncing them.

Wilson received 42 percent of the vote. Taft came in a poor third.

Since it was necessary to include William Jennings Bryan in the government in order to hold the party together, he was made secretary of state. It was mandatory to receive his approval of the Federal Reserve Act before it could be passed. This was obtained after four unsubstantial changes were made in the text of the proposed legislation in order to make it seem that the Fed would be an actual agency of the government.

Whether Bryan was deceived or persuaded to go along with something that was contrary to his long-professed principles, we cannot know now with certainty.

The act was passed on December 23, 1913. Wilson signed it the same day. How all this was accomplished is a long and intricate story, told in detail in my book "The Federal Reserve and Our Manipulated Dollar."*      ●

*$7.95 from Liberty Library, 300 Independence Ave., SE, Washington, D.C. 20003.

# Abolish the Fed

For the first time since the Federal Reserve System was established, a widespread movement is calling for the repeal of the Federal Reserve Act and the replacement of the Federal Reserve System by a Constitutional money system. As an absolute minimum, this will require all currency to be issued by the treasury and all monetary laws and regulations to be made by congressional action and responsibility.

The Fed, as now constituted, is a private institution—even though its board of governors is appointed by the U.S. president with the consent of the Senate. In actual and practical control, there is no government participation. The Fed is totally independent.

Our currency is issued by the 12 member banks of the system. The Fed sets the interest rates, determines the money supply and creates the basis for credit.

Through its Open Market Committee, which operates out of the New York branch alone, it buys and sells government securities in the private market and pays for them either with newly printed Federal Reserve notes or with checks drawn upon the treasury. The Bureau of Engraving and Printing manufactures all the notes the Fed orders. It could issue enough of these next week to pay off the national debt.

Without investing a penny of its own, the Fed was officially in possession of assets totaling $190,128,979,000 as of December 31, 1982. And, since it valued its gold stock at only $42.23 an ounce, with a total value of $11,147,909,000, the true value of its assets was approximately $300 billion.

All this could be legally recovered by the nation by paying the member banks a little more than $1 billion for the stock they hold in the Fed.

It is true that after collecting some $15 billion of interest from its government securities, the Fed repays the surplus to the treasury (after meeting its own expenses out of this income).

## FED'S PURPOSE

The basic purpose of the Fed is not to make current profits for itself, but rather to establish control and enable its member banks and the shadowy insiders who operate them to make enormous profits.

These banks obtain federal securities without any investment of their own funds, use them to collect hundreds of billions of income annually by the swindle known as "fractional reserve banking," a technique by which they obtain liens and mortgages upon private property by issuing checkbook or debt money equal to 10 or more times the cash value of their security assets. They also draw interest from the bonds obtained without investment, and collect and keep this as private profit.

Through the operation of the Open Market Committee, the Fed is able to control interest rates and determine credit.

Each of the 12 member banks has nine directors, of whom three are appointed by the board of governors and the other six elected by the member banks themselves or their stockholders, which gives the latter complete private control.

Note, however, that those appointed by the board are also spokesmen for private interests rather than the public or Congress.

The fact is that we have never had a Constitutional monetary system in this country. When the First United States Bank was established in 1791 under the leadership of Alexander Hamilton, this placed the monetary power in private hands, even as the Federal Reserve System has done since 1913.

Jefferson advocated a program under which the federal debt would be extinguished, the treasury would issue all currency redeemable in specie and under which any emergency or war could be financed without the need for borrowing or increased taxation. But he was defeated by the national and international financiers, who have been in real control of our monetary systems virtually ever since.

**NATIONAL DEBT**

I have long advocated the liquidation of the federal debt. The debt now threatens to reach a point where it will mean the destruction of our culture. The fact is that about half of all federal securities are held by people or entities who never invested in them, but possess them through highly unethical techniques. This half could equitably be expunged by a stroke of a pen without costing the taxpayers anything.

And the remainder could gradually be reduced, even without the personal income tax, if the federal government would cease its expenditures for purposes not permitted or actually forbidden by the Constitution.

Since it seems useless to hope Congress will adopt such statesmanlike measures, but will, instead, continue as long as possible its wild spree of deficit spending, I see nothing ahead except a debt that will become so unmanageable and enormous that eventually our currency must become worthless or the debt must be repudiated in its entirety.

Either alternative would be catastrophic, yet preferable to total national suicide—which might be another possibility.

These options, as I see it, lie in the foreseeable future and well within the life expectancy of most of those now living. Perhaps this will mean the triumph of communism or some form of totalitarian despotism.

For a full discussion of how the Fed was established, how it operates, what its purposes are and how it could be replaced, see my book "The Federal Reserve and Our Manipulated Dollar."*

---

*"The Federal Reserve and Our Manipulated Dollar," by Martin A. Larson, is available for $7.95 from Liberty Library, 300 Independence Ave., SE, Washington, D.C. 20003.

**ALEXANDER HAMILTON**
**. . . Established U.S. Bank.**

# *The Operation of the Fed*

Now that several states have passed memorials demanding that Congress repeal the Federal Reserve Act, any newspaper article criticizing the Fed is answered in long and carefully prepared letters. The Fed is definitely on the defensive.

The line of argument presented by Fed apologists usually follows this pattern:

● Since the members of the Board of Governors are appointed by the president with the advice and consent of the Senate, the Fed is an agency of the government;

● Because it is necessary to free monetary policies from partisan politics, the Fed has necessarily been given a considerable degree of independence;

● Since Congress has exclusive power to coin money and regulate its value, it may Constitutionally confer this function upon another agency;

● The Ninth Circuit Court of Appeals declaration that the Fed banks are private corporations applies only to cases of personal tort and does not invalidate their status as public institutions;

● Since all the interest collected by the Fed on government securities—with the exception of funds used to pay expenses—is returned to the treasury, this proves that the Fed is a governmental institution.

Apologists ignore the fact that the Fed employees do not participate in any federal annuity program; that they are without GS status; that the system pays local real estate taxes on its properties; and that it must pay postage on all its mail. None of these facts applies to any entity that is part of the federal government.

The twin instruments by which the Fed controls American economic and political life are, first, the fractional reserve system of banking. By this member banks are able to create checkbook money for loans equal to 10 or more times the face value of the cash or government securities they hold in their vaults, all of which they have obtained without cost and on which they collect interest.

By this method, they can place mortgages on most of the real estate in the country without actually lending a dime of their own money and collect at least $300 billion of interest annually.

The second great instrument wielded by the Fed is the Open Market Committee, which buys and sells enormous amounts of government securities in the open market and is thus able to dictate the interest rates that shall prevail throughout the economy.

The Fed has power not only to determine rates of interest, but also to determine the amount of credit that shall be available for business or construction; it can also determine the money supply. It could raise interest rates to 40 percent or reduce them to 2. It could print enough Federal Reserve notes at any time to pay off the national debt. It can create inflation or deflation, depression or panics at will. It financed the two world wars and thus increased the national debt to astronomical proportions. It has the power of life and death over the American people and nation.

Ah! but Congress has the power to amend or repeal the Federal Reserve Act at will! But so far it has only amended it at the behest of its masters to increase their power. Only a powerful movement emanating from state legislatures or the people themselves will be sufficient to abolish the Fed or curb its power.

Remember that it will not be sufficient or effective merely to repeal the Federal Reserve Act. The monetary system must be replaced by another which will conform to Constitutional requirements, including, in my opinion, a return to a specie currency—one redeemable in gold or silver. This is not only feasible, but entirely practical.